TILL WE ALL WIN

We Are All a Work in Progress

Kelechukwu Nnabuike Onwukamike (PhD)

Copyright © 2022 by Kelechukwu Nnabuike Onwukamike (PhD)

All rights reserved; no part of this publication may be reproduced in whole or in part, or transmitted in any form or by any means, electronic, mechanical, photocopying, recording or otherwise, without the prior permission of the publisher and the author.

Harmony Publishing

Plot 1 Emmanuel Anabor, Off Mopo Road, United Estate, Sangotedo, Lagos, Nigeria

+2347032212481

publish@harmonypublishing.com.ng

Book cover designers: Dolapo Olawoyin & Nwokafor Chibuzor

Conceptual Editor: Judith Nwatu

ISBN: 9781005590406

Printed in Nigeria

DEDICATION

To the ones who dream, May they find Hope.

ACKNOWLEDGEMENTS

Firstly, I do acknowledge the Almighty God who granted me great grace, wisdom and insight to commence and complete this masterpiece "Till We All Win."

Secondly, I sincerely acknowledge my warrior family, friends, and LinkedIn connections that individually and collectively played a pivotal role in inspiring the book's creation. Also, I am very grateful to my supportive mentees at DEKEMP (Dr KC Mentorship Platform) for their sacrifice of love towards ensuring that this project emerged as a success.

My utmost appreciation goes to Judith Nwatu, who spent countless hours fine-tuning the idea and ensuring that my true intentions were rightly communicated in writing. Also, to Thelma Iheme, who was patient with each bit of the manuscript shared with her for revision, and Precious Orji, who left no stones unturned in the editing part of the manuscript.

Also to Scholastical Gbufor who reviewed the manuscript on short notice, and my dear friend Naledi Mashiane, who tutored me on the best way to communicate my experiences in this book correctly, I remain gratefully grateful.

In a special way, I acknowledge my older brother, Engineer Marvelous Onwukamike, for his in-depth review of the book, which ultimately gave it the touch of perfection needed. I am eternally grateful to my parents Evang. & Mrs Edwin

Chukwuka Onwukamike. My siblings Dr Hillary, Nkechi, Uche, Okwudiri, Gozie and Tochi, for being the most supportive family anyone could wish for.

Last but not least, my son Delight: I am immensely grateful to God for the gift of you and the genuine love we share which daily strengthens me to pursue and conquer. And to everyone who would delight in reading this book, I am grateful and appreciate you greatly.

Thank you one, thank you all.

Kelechukwu Nnabuike Onwukamike

Frankfurt, Germany

5th Dec. 2021

CONTENTS

DEDICATION iii
ACKNOWLEDGEMENTS v
CONTENTS vii
Foreword by Dr Taiwo Michael (Founder MT Scholarship) xi
LinkedIn connections wish for *"Till We All Win"* xiii
TESTIMONIALS FOR THE BOOK, *"Till We All Win"* xvii
PREFACE xxiii
INTRODUCTION xxv
THEME 1: *The Charge* 1
1. It Is Too Late, Forget About First Position 3
   2. What the Heart Seeks: A Teenager's Love Story 6
   3. Believe or Pursue: My High School Experience at GBHS Kumbo 11
   4. Impossible Says I'm Possible: My Undergraduate Experience at FUTO 19
   5. Tell My Teacher: He Made Me Careful to Succeed 26
   6. Is Education a Scam? 30
THEME 2: *Beyond Physical Appearance* 39
   7. Worth More than Our Looks: Someone Like Me 41
   8. Respect Open Doors: My Second-Year Internship Experience 45
   9. Mother the Situation: Set the Pace 49
      9.1 Mr "Your Fahrkarte" 54
   10. Kindness is Colourful 57
THEME 3: *Work In Progress* 61

11. No One's Head is Touching the Ceiling 63
12. The Road Travelled 66
13. You Will Surprise Yourself 72

THEME 4: *Life's Imagination versus Reality* 75
14. Take Me to School 77
15. Not All Figured Out 80
16. Experiences: What Counts is What You Do with Them ... 91
17. Delay Can Be a Redirection 95
    17.1 Not over, till it is over 103

THEME 5: *Persistence & Resilience* 107
18. Rebel intent; life lessons learnt 109
19. Thanks, but I Will Take My Chances 115
20. Not For Less 118

THEME 6: *The Light in Failure* 121
21. What Does Failure Mean to You? 123
22. Lose the Battle, Win the War 126

THEME 7: *The Scholars Ship* 131
23. Process over Result 133
24. Scholarship: For Me, Or Not For Me 138
25. After The One Yes 146
26. Writing It Down: What I Did Differently As a Student ... 152

THEME 8: *Direction over Speed* 157
27. No Rush: The Danger of Frustration Induced Decision . 159
28. Not What I Am Looking For: I Am Not Studying Industrial Chemistry 163

THEME 9: *Seize the moment* 167
29. What Is In Your Hand? 169

30. Brain Gain, Not Brain Drain 172

THEME 10: *Hope; the reason for tomorrow* 177

    31. Now or Later: Adapting & Thriving In a New Environment 179

    32. No Victim Card to Play 186

    33. Lose Not Sight of the Bigger Picture: The Domino Effect 190

    34. Not Easy: Experience from My PhD Journey 196

THEME 11: *Humility in Success* 203

    35. Humility Can Be Learnt 205

    36. Remember Yesterday 209

THEME 12: *Till We All Win* 213

    37. Not Again: The Experience That Redefined Winning for Me 215

    38. Where My Loyalty Lies 219

    39. The Place of Coaching and Mentoring 223

    40. The Culture of Togetherness: DEKEMP and Beyond 228

AFTERWORD: *My Hope* 235

Foreword by Dr Taiwo Michael (Founder MT Scholarship)

I have always been fascinated by inequality. Why do some people make it, and others don't? Why do some end up poor and bankrupt, whereas some others from the same place born around the same time go on to become wildly successful? There are several answers to these ageless questions but none more important than mindset. What separates the haves and have nots, the contenders from the pretenders, the winners from the rest cannot be measured by a ruler, weighed on a scale, or sized by the eye for it is a potent invisible force that creates the visible result. I am talking about the quality of the thinking inside each person. Solomon, the wisest man who ever lived, puts it best, "As he thinks in his heart, so is he." (Prov. 23:7)

Fortunately, our minds are like muscles that can be trained. The more we discipline them to process information and thoughts in a certain way, in the direction of success, the more they work for us and bring to pass the things we really want. This is where this excellent book you are holding comes in. See the author, Dr. Kelechukwu Onwukamike, as your mind trainer and *Till We All Win* as the curriculum. As you read story after story of how he achieved feat after feat in the face of daunting odds, I want you to see a common thread in all of this. He first won in his mind before it was manifested in his life. Your story can be the same.

But *Till We All Win* doesn't end at personal victory. Its ambition is bigger: create a winning network. A *win-win* disposition is an intangible attribute that manifests in tangible ways, and by making this its central message, *Till We All Win* passes from the realm of the merely good books to a great piece of art. True greatness lies in making others achieve it. The developed world understands this, but the developing world is yet to trust this idea. The former understands that *till we all win, no one has truly won* and goes about creating a superstructure where people can thrive. The latter has the *I-pass-my-neighbor* mentality and inadvertently form a society where many think of life as a zero-sum game i.e. someone needs to lose for another to win. *Till We All Win* will correct your thinking.

It is hard to choose a favourite chapter. They are all really good. I encourage you to take your time with this book and come back to it often when you need inspiration. The primary audience of this book are students looking for scholarships, but it is so good that it applies to anybody. After all, winning is not only for students. I want to thank the author, Dr. Kelechukwu Onwukamike, for distilling years of wisdom into the following pages. Do yourself a favour. Buy this book. And share what you learn with others. Keep sharing till we all win.

Truly yours,

Michael Taiwo, PhD

Founder of the Michael Taiwo Scholarships

LinkedIn connections wish for "*Till We All Win*"

Aside from my desire to share knowledge and experience for impact purposes through a book, I also believed it would be a good tool in addressing most of the questions I always received from my esteemed LinkedIn connections. So following my decision to begin writing in early 2021, I took an extra step by creating a LinkedIn post where I gave an insight on the book title and goal.

In the LinkedIn post, I urged my connections comprising of fellow professionals, scholars, mentees to comment on the post. And most importantly, give feedback indicating areas they would like me to address and questions they need me to answer inside the book.

In reply, I received loads of comments and feedback. Amazingly, I captured the comments and questions to honour the respondents and bring their desires and wishes, alongside mine, to life in the book. Thus it is safe to say that "Till we all win" is an unconventional book for us and by us.

#tillweallwin

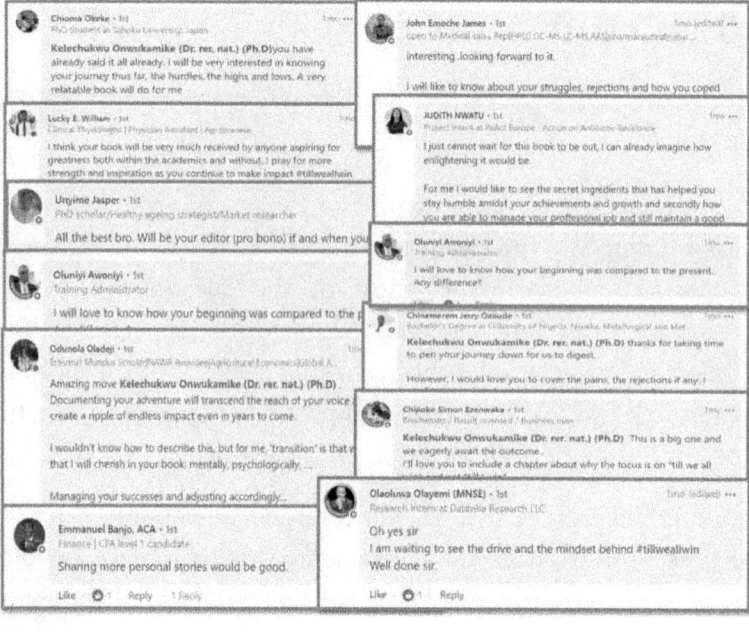
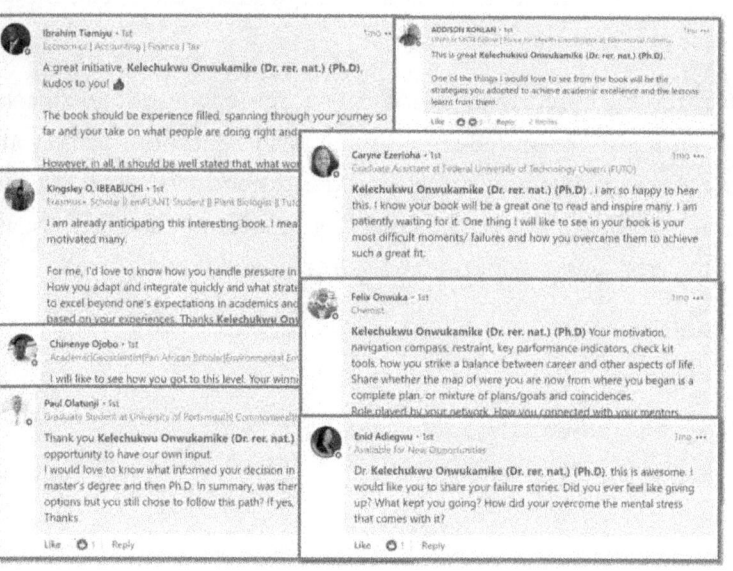

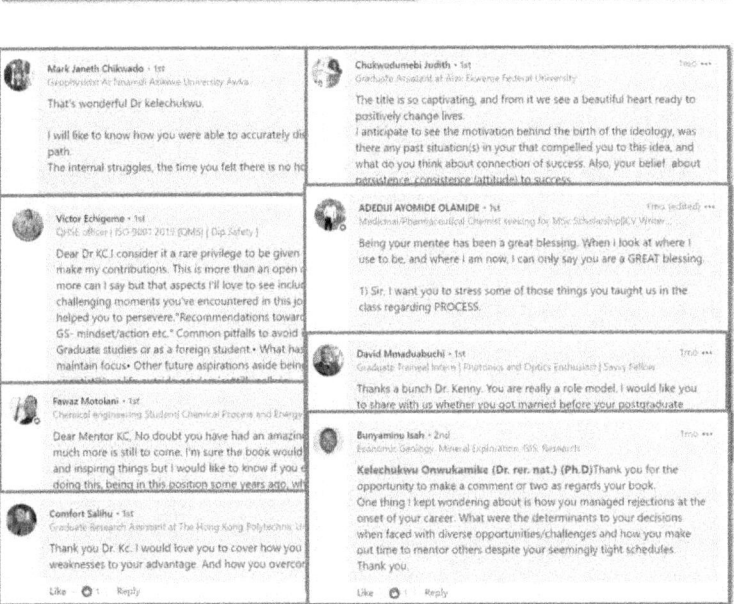

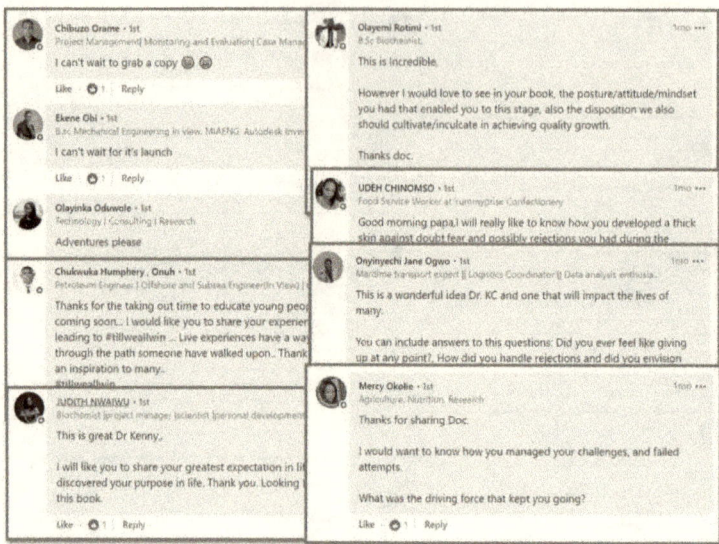

TESTIMONIALS FOR THE BOOK, *"Till We All Win"*

Till we all win is one book I will recommend to any youth, young adults and young professionals who are just starting their career. After reading several chapters of this text, I must confess that it is truly inspirational. Most importantly, I couldn't agree less with Dr. KC that #tillweallwin is a philosophy that is rooted in a growth mindset. #Tillweallwin X-rayed many life nuggets any prospective life winner desires to use to journey the path of success. This text brings a constant reminder to us that "Life truly promises us nothing, so we can either play the blame game or navigate this ship to the destination of our dream. Yes. Life promises us NOTHING, but we are EVERYTHING marvellous and EVERYTHING beautifully made by God." All practical experiences shared in this text were relatable because they were real life experiences. As I was reading, I saw myself in the light of Dr KC´s life and many journeys. Indeed, *Till We All Win* is a great title for the book. Therefore I recommend this book for all to read.

Wilfred Asuquo, MS (*Agile Coach, Product Owner, Business & Data Analyst, Certified John Maxwell Coach, USA*)

In *Till We All Win*, Dr Onwukamike records his personal experiences in order to inspire future generations. His tone is one that shows us he is a hard worker full of humility who has a deep desire to serve those around him. The reader feels both the struggles and the triumphs as he crafts the words on the page in a way that draws you into his personal story. Dr Kelechukwu Onwukamike shares lessons from his life and teaches us that the most important thing in any circumstance is not whether it is good or bad but rather our reaction to the situation that makes all the difference. The story is ultimately about HOPE and TRANSFORMATION for anyone willing to learn.

Denise Grindstaff (*International Relations Specialist, USA*)

Till We All Win is a book of inspiring personal stories that exemplify resilience, optimism and purposeful living. I was particularly intrigued and indeed motivated by the selfless mindset reflected by the author in every chapter of the book. In his despair, he refused to quit. Rather he constantly kept faith with the journey while checking every required box in the process of attaining greatness. The younger generation aspiring to achieve a set goal despite all odds would find strength and encouragement by reading this book. Dr. KC is a blessing to our teaming youths as he continues to give his all in helping them to navigate through their career journeys.

Victor Ogunmola (*Geoscientist, Human Builder, Mentor, Volunteer @ i-Scholar Initiative*)

Kelechukwu Onwukamike's *Till We All* is a testimonial to the fundamental belief of the cake being big enough for all of us. It's a great read for everyone who is truly interested in personal growth and growing others. Till we all win!

Sven Seibert (*Procter & Gamble R&D Haircare Packaging Director, Germany*)

Life is a journey, and everyone has a sole responsibility to work his/her journey. As we journey through life, we gather personal experiences filled with lessons, hardships, heartaches, happiness, celebrations and special moments that will ultimately lead us to our destination.

Till We All Win documents *the* journey *of Dr* Onwukamike. The whole book is permeated with stories about academic excellence through a growth mindset. In particular, I enjoyed the simplicity, humility, and vividness demonstrated in this very insightful book. This book will provide students worldwide with advice regarding networking, graduate school scholarships, professional guidance, and much more.

Prof. Olaniyi A. Fawole (*Professor, University of Johannesburg, South Africa*)

We live in a day and age where we are unapologetic about celebrating black excellence. We are intentional about winning and reaching emancipation; therefore, allow yourself to get mentally stimulated by this incredibly written book that'll change your life and have a concrete impact. Not only will you be challenged mentally, but you'll also get inspired to want to change your idiosyncrasies, demeanour and your conventional nor orthodoxical ways of thinking. Dr KC breaks down the tools of having a winning mindset in this incredibly written memoir inspired by his vision, "Till We All Win". In the words of Thomas Jefferson, "If you want something you've never had, you have to do something you've never done before", therefore by being conscious of how you think, you'll train your subconscious mind to be selective. Your mind is like a garden; what are you feeding it? Dr KC has succinctly re-applied the concept of "fixed or growth mindset", where he gives a detailed analysis and a crystal distinction betwixt the two. He further emphasised the notion that life is "Not all figured out" but full of uncertainties; therefore, it is up to us to comprehend that we are all a work in progress. Rejection is a mother to none. Whether you're opulent, successful, educated, poor, etc., it's inevitable. It can happen to anybody. In the author's words, I quote, "Pause and ask yourself what exactly is the lesson behind, or you beat yourself over spilt milk over and over again?" Do you take rejection as a re-direction, or do you easily give up? Either way, the law of attraction responds to your thoughts. You are what you think; you are your thoughts—having a winning mindset all starts from the mind. Education doesn't necessarily mean attaining certification but also plays a pivotal role in changing how we should think critically and progressively. This book shares a perspective to the infamous question, "Is Education is a scam?". This is a conversation that is of paramount significance. This book doesn't choose; it is for everybody. #Tillweallwin is a movement, a mantra, and a way of living till we ultimately win. Dr KC is holding the torch for everyone; he's holding firmly to the ladder so that we can climb TILL WE ALL WIN. In the words of Ms Lauryn Hill: "Black people should write their own stories", well, I agree!

Enjoy reading.

Naledi Alexis Mashiane (*Avid reader, PanAfricanist, Sales Consultant at Levati Water South Africa)*

Till We All Win is not just a book, but a life guide that entails in depth principles and real-life experiences to aid everyone to successfully navigate through the sequences of life. Kelechukwu meticulously details the importance of looking beyond self-win, and having a We All Win mindset.

In a generation where everyone is focused on achieving great feats and Heights for themselves, to glorify their efforts, this books debunks that mentality and encourages the reader to look beyond self- actualisation, and focus on lifting others up.

Indubitably, I will suggest this book to everyone! I strongly believe that as humans, we are not just created to live our own lives, but rather to impact the lives of others through our purpose.

Maame De-Heer (*Policy Analyst at Government of Canada)*

Till We All Win is a raw, original, and highly inspiring masterpiece, written from a wealth of lived experiences and not from unproven theories. The author, Dr. Kelechukwu (Dr. KC, as he is fondly called), clearly demonstrated how he reinvented himself, made those who underrated him eat their own words, and overcame recurring challenges to live his dreams. I, therefore, recommend this book to students, graduates, professionals and even parents, as it contains a lot of wisdom for living and thriving, including lessons on academic tenacity in discouraging terrains. Dr. KC showed in the book how to be motivated by challenges, rather than being frustrated by them, and cited true stories from his past to support his claims. Conclusively, the book contains values and strategies that could be adopted to live a life of excellence and significance, and of giving-back, for according to his mantra, "until we have all won, no one has truly won."

Babajide Milton Macaulay, Ph.D. (*Lecturer, Department of Biology, Federal University of Technology, Akure (FUTA), Nigeria, Founder, iLLUMANIA (www.illumania.org).*

This enjoyable book is the real meaning of "your success is my success."

Kenny leverages his life experience, academic skill on the African continent and overseas, to teach us the power of mentoring and inclusive mindset to help the mentees unleash their full potential.

Till we all win is undeniably an important stuff to read! Something that finally relates a vivid intellectual history to see beyond the lenses that stand in front of us and help embrace the culture of equity, networking, confidence and mutual support till we all win, together.

Moussa Yattara *(E2E R&D Surface Care Wipes Leader, Procter & Gamble Belgium)*

Till We All Win gave me unique insights into what motivates Kenny and what actions he has taken personally towards making the world a better place for us all. I appreciated learning about his childhood, and how he approached each new challenge with a growth mindset – not being a victim of circumstance, but taking control and holding himself accountable thereby leading to his accomplishments. This has clearly translated into his personal passion to enable others to do the same, bringing out their best through mentorship and scholarship opportunities.

Keep up the good works.

Michael Britt *(R&D Senior Director, Haircare Europe, Germany)*

If you're a dreamer of bigger better things for the world and for yourself - this book is for you. We live in a society that sacrifices the many for the one - something I believe we are gradually unlearning.

Kenny's book and philosophy helps us reengage with the truth that the success of one cannot occur without the support and input of another.

Society is just beginning to relearn this powerful idea of leveraging the power of community & networks for incredible success - in one's health, career and business.

Love Kenny's teachings and his powerful philosophy!

Zanele Njapha *(The Unlearning Lady, Unlearning Expert & Transitions Facilitator, TomorrowToday Global, South Africa)*

PREFACE
Till we all win, we are all a work in progress

The idea of considering success beyond self-actualisation cropped up in my early childhood. I was steady passionate about sharing my knowledge with others. More so, it was a win-win situation for me since I learned even more by so doing.

Oftentimes, I wondered if the same ideology applied to everyone and what the world would look like if it did. So, in my quest to unravel convincing answers to these sort of puzzling questions in my head, I birth newer questions instead. Hence can we all win? How practical or feasible is a collective win, especially one achieved through assisting other people learn or improve in knowledge and skills. How realistic is an all-win situation? Or it is more of a folk tale?

On a second note, questions like: What does winning mean? When have we truly won? How far can we go to win? And, at what point do we stop being a work in progress? Alongside many other questions not outlined here were the typical subjects of discussion on my LinkedIn page after I began the #tillweallwin hashtag in 2019. Interestingly, these questions and conversations inspired me to take the next bold step into sharing my life journey through this book.

For me, till we all win is a philosophy rooted in a growth mindset that recognises that a win for one does not translate to a loss for another. At the forefront of this philosophy is the ideology that "the pie" is not fixed and life is not a zero-sum game. Furthermore, it reiterates that everyone can get their share without making the others go hungry.

I am pretty positive that our perspective of life would take a better turn if we realised that one's win does not stop another. With this mindset, a piece of information that would most likely help the stranger right beside us is not hoarded or withheld because it doesn't benefit us. Unlike the quest to be the only one-eyed man in the kingdom of the blind just to be crowned king, the importance of an "all-win community" is acknowledged, and the stress of being the "only one" is lifted.

Therefore, a definite "yes" answer to the question: can we all win, is only possible with us all, embracing an unbiased, supportive role to one another with the understanding that no one wholly wins without another, which is the reason why we remain work in progress after all.

Taking a few steps backwards, I'd like to ask a pertinent question: does buying into the ideology of "till we all win, we are all a work in progress" guarantee us a life of promise?

INTRODUCTION
This is life, nothing is promised

"Nothing in life is promised." This response is my candid answer to the earlier question, "does buying into the ideology of *till we all win, we are all a work in progress* guarantee us a life of promise?" and I will explain why.

Our past, present, future uncertainties and many more are contentions we eventually have to deal with as we go through life. From my experience, I realised that the most difficult fact to accept about life is the uncertainties that come with it. When I look at the different stages of human growth, the stage considered to be the most important is age 18 and above, that is, the legal age in most countries. By law, we can be held responsible for our actions at this age and become the decisions we make or do not make. Therefore, I consider it a point of no return, where we can either blame our upbringing, and background or look beyond our circumstances to chart a unique course for our lives. Though not as simple as it may seem, at this point, each of us should come to terms with the fact that life promises us nothing we are not determined to either nurture or pursue.

What about our parents? One might ask. Don't they owe us a responsibility to provide, guide and watch over us till we are ready to be on our feet? No, they do not owe us anything. What about our circumstances, place of birth and the limitations of our backgrounds? Can't we blame these uncontrollable factors for denying us the future of our dreams? As unlikely as it might sound, we cannot blame our circumstances for limiting us. Even if we choose to blame them, what use, or difference would it make? Until we come to that realisation that life promises us nothing, we might remain in bad shape longer than we could ever imagine. Again, I would say that going through life with an expectation of an all smooth ride is a recipe for frustration mixed with rage. However, if we choose to push through, the sun eventually rises.

As an individual, my faith in Christ Jesus forms the foundation on which I chart into the uncertainties that come with life. When challenged with a harrowing experience, I find comfort through hope in Christ Jesus with an absolute trust that He will neither leave nor forsake me. Therefore, I recognise challenging situations as a necessary experience to prepare me for my future.

As we walk through the different phases of our lives, it helps us to recognize that we are created different and our paths are unique. That way, we are not swayed by unnecessary competition.

I do agree that we live in the social media age where most people promote the fake it till you make it philosophy. An era where smiling faces and luxurious lifestyles are stage-managed to belong and please, which sadly impels some other people to feel unworthy and less of themselves. Should it then become the norm? I do not think so.

Rather than slide into depression as many have, trying to please the world that is never satisfied, we all can do better by living the precious and unique life gifted to us by God. Live first!

"Once there is life, there is hope." HOPE, the four-letter words that drove me to establish a mentorship platform, is a crucial enabler that encourages us to press on till we become the reality of our dreams. As humans, we must understand that hope cannot be built on vain wishes, neither will it appear out of nothing, but from the point of sincereness and inward reflection of being truthful to ourselves first and the world at large.

This is life, where nothing is promised, and each human will have to act their part on the stage using the props given and improvising on those not provided.

In summary, this is what life is to me; a stage where we get the rare privilege to showcase our role and, in essence, leave a lasting impact by how we choose to handle the uncertainties that come our way. Let us remember that our life is a gift, and we cannot afford to cherish it any less. As we walk through life, let us be reminded that no true joy grows outside of ourselves; true happiness is from within us. Since this is the case, we can CHOOSE to be happy and be RESPONSIBLE for our happiness. To the moments of uncertainties that come with life, we can choose how we react to everything life throws at us. Yes, life does not promise us anything, BUT we can decide how we ACT towards what life challenges us with on the path to realising our dreams. How we handle these challenges makes us UNIQUE, and that's how we can chart the course towards a fulfilling life. Life indeed promises us nothing, so we can either play the game of blame or navigate this ship to the destination of our dream.

Yes, life promises us nothing, but we can CHOOSE intentionally to nurture or pursue a life that sees beyond self-actualisation.

Yes, life promises us nothing, but we can OPT to continue being a work in progress till we all win.

Yes, life promises us NOTHING, but we are EVERYTHING marvellous and EVERYTHING beautifully made by God.

THEME 1:
The Charge

1
It Is Too Late, Forget About First Position

The above statement was supported by an even stronger one; "you cannot". It is perhaps one of the earliest memories of my years in primary school. For the records, at the time, I was enrolled at the Catholic School Ndzegwev, Kumbo-Cameroon and in Primary Four. Following the close of the term, our teacher carefully handed over our results, I unfolded mine to see, and my position was 5th. When I got home, the first person I met was my older cousin and she inquired of my report card which I handed over. After glancing through, she returned it to me with an indifferent look on her face. As I was about to take my leave, she said "5th position, no surprise. Considering that your best performance had been 3rd position , we cannot expect you to ever take 1st position since you are now moving to higher classes that are even more difficult. Anyways you have tried, well done."

The Charge

Typical of an African kid who would strongly believe as told provided it came from an elderly person, I took her word for it. However, it worried me because I knew I was giving my best to study and desired better grades.

When I got to primary five, I worked so hard to achieve a better performance than my best at the point which was 3rd position. Shockingly to me, I ended up with 8th position instead. When my cousin saw my results, I remember her looking at me with an "I told you so" gaze. Miraculously, when I got to my Primary six, I was able to achieve a 2nd position. I was really happy to have broken my own records. This encouraged me to aim for the 1st position. The same 1st position that my childhood friend had maintained from our Primary one. With my Primary six performance, I felt I could perhaps have a chance at 1st position.

The next class, Primary seven, which was supposed to host my big break, had barely begun when my dad decided to transfer me to another school named the Presbyterian School Kumbo. As if that was not enough, the school housed a generation of brainbox. Hence, where was I to begin and end with my 1st position quest? "It is well" happened to it, I reasoned. When I got to this new school, I didn't remember trying to do anything different, I studied hard as I had always done, with very little expectation. I topped my class and finally got 1st position! I could not contain my joy! It was indeed a big deal going from a first time 2nd position in Primary five to the achieving the 1st position in a much tougher class (Primary seven) in a more competitive school.

My cousin sister was no longer with us, but I ensured writing her a letter stating that I had taken 1st position. I also wrote that I would maintain the 1st position for the remaining two terms and graduate amongst the best in my school and region in the First School Leaving and Common Entrance Examinations.

And that, I did.

I achieved what I was told I could not. Hurrah!

This experience made me realise that the only one who could or can stop me, is me. It doesn't matter what people think or say of me. My main concern should be to keep improving myself.

People often do not try to limit you because they hate or do not like your growth. In my opinion, the concern or limitation they place on you comes from their experiences or what they may have accepted of themselves. If my effort did not yield a good fruit as you have read, I would most likely be here selling the same "you cannot" narrative. Therefore, my advice remains that you take every feedback you get, assimilate, and pick up what will help you grow. Whereas I spent my earlier childhood trying to disprove my cousin sister, this is not the best approach. Instead, please do what you must do because it is crucial for your self-development and growth, not necessarily because you are trying to prove a point to someone else.

The quest for 1st position got me what I wanted, I now know better how to define "the why" behind any pursuit. Nonetheless, if you choose to challenge a "forget the first position" scenario in your life, do not for any reason forget that the competition is with no one but yourself.

2
What the Heart Seeks: A Teenager's Love Story

The 'firsts' are usually memorable; perhaps because they are new and we don't have any references to compare with. For example, first walk as a child, first day in school, first love, first kiss, and even first love story. Indeed everything has a beginning, and my love story is no different. My LinkedIn connections had wished that I share my "love adventures." As I look back in retrospect, nothing comes close to my first love story. It is absolutely unique and has remained indelible in my mind because I grew up very shy around girls outside my family. My shyness towards girls was so bad that simply attaching my name to any girl's name was enough to make me cry and even wail. My older sister knew this trick so well that she wouldn't hesitate to use it anytime I claimed to be a big boy. When I got into secondary school at PCHS Kumbo in Cameroon, it didn't take long before some of my female classmates noticed. For example, I wouldn't sit with any girl, I wouldn't stay close to any girl, and unless necessary, I hardly spoke to any girl outside my immediate family circle. Having noticed my shyness towards girls, two of my female classmates decided to "torment" me one day in class. They both decided to sit on each end of the desk, thereby trapping me in the middle. All effort to escape failed, and I had only one choice; hide my face in my palms and cry. I can still remember their laughter and the laughter of my classmates.

Knowing this side of me, I didn't imagine I would one day feel the 'love thing' some of my friends were already talking about until one fateful day in Form 2. I was 14 at the time and started noticing I felt something different for a particular female classmate. My earliest memory of this "love feeling" started with watching her walk into the class. I am not sure what made this particular day different because we had been classmates for over two years. But, on that day, when my eyes "opened", I noticed her elegance, black beauty, and sweet voice, which left me speechless. "Haa, is this how this 'love thing' is?" I said to myself. At that moment, something in my heart skipped; a feeling I couldn't describe rushed through my body and I struggled to keep my composure. During this period, I noticed that I didn't feel "well" when I don't see her. So I began building up the muscle to keep conversations with her. In no time, she felt comfortable coming to me for help with her studies. It didn't take long for people to start noticing us studying together. Spending time together continued for the next two years. This caused all of our friends to think we were dating, even though we weren't. Until one day, I decided that it was time to let my heart's desire known to her, but I couldn't muster the courage to say "I love you." "It is better to let things be as they are," I said to myself. At least, in this phase I can safely assume that she feels the same way about me than

The Charge

asking and finding out otherwise. My brain won over my heart so I didn't tell her.

A few months later, the bombshell dropped. One of my friends told me he was interested in her. Oh boy, I barely slept that night. Interested? Same girl I have been 'wooing' for almost three years? I couldn't believe it. To make matters worse, I remember seeing them together after an evening class, walking so close to each other that I felt my heart would disappear if it continued beating at that rate. So I decided it was either now or never. I don't want her to blame it on me not telling her. So, I decided to make my move by writing a love letter. I pulled all the grammar tricks up my sleeve and used as many adorning adjectives as I could. It was such a ride. I cannot recall how many times I had to start rewriting until I eventually got the one that captured my feeling perfectly. Since I am not taking any chances, I concluded the letter by asking her to be my girlfriend. After writing, it quickly dawned on me that I didn't factor the courage it would take to deliver the letter in my decision-making process, and the fact that she might say no. So, I kept the letter for an entire week, waiting for the strength to take the next step. Finally, on the eve of my 17th birthday, I decided to damn the consequences. I sent the letter to her through another female classmate alongside some lovely biscuits. Just turning seventeen, I couldn't have imagined the events that followed after making such a move. I expected she would reply with the same urgency I had when I wrote the letter. Alas, it was nothing like that. The first day after was the longest. I waited for her reply and got nothing. The same thing happened the next day and the day after and the day after that. Days slowly rolled into a week and nothing yet but we saw each other in class everyday. It was nerve-racking! Worse, she acted as though she didn't receive the letter. I had to go back to the person I sent it through to check if she really delivered my message. "Yes, of course, I did," she replied. I was gradually losing my mind and felt disappointed in myself for making the move. I couldn't focus on my studies and exams were fast approaching. My brain reminded me to face my book and forget about the 'love thing'. After all, my brain did warn me not to make the move. But I just couldn't shake off the feeling. My heart had successfully hijacked my brain and I was in limbo.

It took until the end of the second week before I got a reply from her. Unlike me, she was bold enough to hand it over to me herself. I kept the letter so secure that anyone who saw her handing it over to me would have thought this was a secret that could bring the world to her knees if revealed. I couldn't wait to leave the class and go to someplace quiet to digest its content. I finally got my break and quickly made my way to a quiet spot. I couldn't wait to read the letter word by word. Instead, I anxiously scanned the entire letter, looking for the phrase 'I love you'. Not seeing any, with my heart pounding like a sprint runner, I read the reply to my first love letter, line by line. When I was done, the tears that had started dropping after reading the first paragraph had arrived on my lips. I could taste it and it was bitter. As I swallowed my bitter tears, I tore the letter and struggled to sleep, hoping never to set my eyes on her again. Unfortunately, sleep was only a temporary fix. I had to wake up to the harsh reality that the only girl I had ever loved doesn't love me back. In her words, "I will be very willing to be your girlfriend when we get to the university, not now." Even though it seemed hopeful, I was sure this is the same as saying NO. The only solution was to disappear but then I realized GCE O-level exam was getting closer and that meant I had to keep being her study buddy. This made the situation even more difficult to bear. She must have noticed the constraint in our friendship because she suddenly decided to limit the chance of us seeing each other.

When the exams were over, and as I took my leave from PCHS Kumbo, I knew that it would be a helluva challenge to try this 'love of a thing' again. I was comforted that I would be leaving for Nigeria to proceed with my education. So it was a huge shock when my parents changed their plans of me moving back to Nigeria and instead wanted me to resume at my former school. Hell no, I am not going back to that school. So, I rebelled against my parents, as captured in another chapter of this book.

"So what does the heart seek?" My brain asked my heart. There was a long silence and till this day my brain still remember this teenager´s first love story.

When I think about other experiences that "charged" me to give my best towards academic pursuit & excellence, I strongly believe this heartbreak contributed because it was obvious 'book' was all I had.

3
Believe or Pursue: My High School Experience at GBHS Kumbo

First impressions, they say, matter. The reason we are always encouraged to make it worthwhile. Also inclusive in this light is the first-hand knowledge we have, receive or believe of something or someplace.

Within the first week of my resumption at the Government Bilingual High School, Kumbo (GBHS), I had an interesting encounter with an old friend. One sunny afternoon after school, I was on my way home when we met, and after we exchanged pleasantries, he was kind enough to advise me about the school. Since he was an alumnus of the school, it meant a lot to me, so I paid apt attention.

"Young man, I learned you are now a student of GBHS Kumbo," he said.

"Yes, I am," I replied.

"I also understand that you are brilliant, but you see, GBHS is a tougher school than your previous school. You are most

The Charge

likely to disappear in the crowd, and very easily too," he added, and that was it. He left me to my thoughts and went his way.

I do not recall thanking him, however I was grateful he saw the need to advise me. He knew better than me, and his advice came from experience. Not again! I muttered as I pondered how and what I was going to do. Sudden fear gripped me as I began to ponder on my next steps.

A little recollection of the "first position" experience I previously described best translates how I felt after the conversation. "Do not tell me I have to prove myself again", I said to myself. Is it even necessary, and can the "you cannot" drama seize already? I guess it never will.

Note that this senior friend of mine meant no harm. He only could not see the reasons why I left my previous school where I was a star to another new school where I would get lost in the crowd of high excelling students. On my end, I had no prior history or knowledge of the academic excellence GBHS students exuded. My decision to school at GBHS was born out of rebellion against my parents for not allowing me return to Nigeria after my secondary school education.

Forward to my experience at GBHS Kumbo; it only took the first term for me to make meaning out of what my senior friend said about the school. Indeed, GBHS Kumbo had very brilliant students. I remember my first test results vividly. It was Pure Mathematics, and I scored 27/50, a pass mark, yes, but what was there to celebrate? Many people had over 40. The highest a 46/50. Sadly, my close group of friends failed the test but were interestingly comforted with my score. They even saw the need to congratulate me for scaling through.

They also wondered why I was indifferent rather than happy. This low pass score would have been the highest score in my previous school which further highlights the exceptional brilliance of GBHS students. Remember that I had left my previous school, PCHS Kumbo as the best student with an overall score of 24/33 points (passed ten papers out of 11 in the GCE O-level examination). Whereas in GBHS Kumbo, at least ten students passed all their papers (11/11) in the same O-level GCE with 30/33 points. I recall a student who made straight 11 A's (33/33). What was there to say again? It's over, *mbok!* It was crystal clear to me at this point that I was in for a tough one. The real question was no longer about getting "lost" but how soon it was to happen.

As other test results got released, I lost my count and record of position. I was nowhere, so no need. Despite all that was going on, which reminded me of the conversation with my senior friend, one thing remained unchanging: the promise I made to myself to pursue the best result with my best effort, carefully avoiding excuses.

On the closure of the first term, the school observed a customary activity that involved calling out students who had the best results from 1st to 3rd position at the assembly ground. Though the activity was new to me, and I was happy to learn about it, it still made me somewhat sad. There was no room for the 5th position I had. Whilst the 1st position average was 16/20, mine was 13.5/20. Funny enough, a particular set of students maintained the top positions all through first year of high school called lower-sixth. Even my journey to the 5th position I had was an intense one. None of the students slacked even a bit. I literally toiled to get to that position. Nonetheless I believed it was doable to achieve a better position, so I continued to push.

When we got to the second year of high school called Upper-sixth, I fueled my hard work by creating a study group. An efficient approach for achieving collective wins which I discovered in my secondary school. Not to worry, I would give more details on the study group (tutorial) approach much later in the book. For this scenario, the study group consisted of my four friends and I. The custom was to share different topics and meet after school each day and on weekends to study. We studied together in preparation for our mock examination, which preceded the final Advanced Level GCE examinations. The scheduled mock exam was for end of February 2007 i.e. the next year so our tutorial ended at the close of school in December 2006. As the holiday begun, the only thing on my mind was the exam. It is safe to say that I did not celebrate Christmas in 2006 because all I did was study. On Christmas day, 25th December, I was locked up in my room all day studying; no Christmas emotions of any sort crossed my mind. My mum understood *the assignment*, as Nigerians would say, so she served my Christmas rice, chicken, drinks and *chin-chin* on my reading table. The goal was to win or nothing, so I had to go extra. I studied over 14 hours daily for the entire three weeks' school break.

When we resumed in January 2007, I broke down with a critical illness. It was so bad; I feared death for the first time. I was completely down and could not open a book or go to school. After two weeks away from school, I insisted on going even though I had not fully recovered as I could no longer hold down my frustration. I had missed so many vital classes that would have helped prepare me for the mock exam as well as my after school tutorials with my friends. I just had to go back, so my parents decided to give it a chance. Unfortunately, it turned out sour for everyone as I collapsed while on our way to school. *Las las*, I gave in to waiting until I was fully recovered and fit to go back to school.

When I finally resumed, it was barely two weeks to the mock examinations. Thanks to my study group, I could catch up with most topics taught in my absence. The D-day: the mock examination day finally came. I sat for five subjects (Pure Mathematics, Further Mathematics, Physics, Biology, and Chemistry). I gave it my all but still felt like I could have done better except for the ill-health.

A few weeks later, I was seated in class when my study group partner and friend ran into the class shouting my name; "KC, KC come and see." What could be making her so excited this afternoon? "The mock results are out," she finally found her breath to tell me. I leapt from my seat and ran behind her to the academic building, where the results were pasted. The place was filled to the brim with students as they struggled to check their results. I squeezed my way through the surging crowd to the front. To my utmost surprise, and I guess to everyone else, my name was first on the list. I was the only one who passed all five subjects with the overall best grades. Many students who came to check the list with the usual expectation of seeing the familiar names that were called consistently on the assembly ground had their mouths open in shock after reading Onwukamike Kelechukwu Nnabuike as the overall best student.

Who is this guy? Someone asked. Another from my class pointed at me, and I could feel all their eyes on me. A friend came to me after and said, "this is only a mock examination and will not be repeated at the final examinations," to which I replied, "we see how that goes." In my mind, I knew the success called for another fierce study. Not only to retain the first position but also to inspire my study mates the more to believe achieving the same feat was possible.

In no time, the long-awaited final exam period came—the GCE examination held in June. I took all my papers, including Biology and Chemistry's practical sections. After the exams, we had about six weeks of holidays while awaiting the result announcement that usually happened in August.

Time flew to August. On the 14th, to be precise, we heard rumours that the GCE results were out, and it was so eventually. In Cameroon, August was well known by all and sundry as the GCE result month. According to the examination centres, the names of successful students were called on the national radio and also printed on special editions of the National Daily Newspaper to emphasise how remarkable the period was. On confirmation that it was no rumour, I called my senior from my previous school in Buea (where the results are usually first released). I asked for his help to check my result and he agreed. This task was not supposed to take long, but hours passed, and I did not hear from him. I became utterly restless and nervous. I was not worried about failing the exam (which meant not passing two out of the five subjects) but was more concerned about my overall performance.

When I finally got a call from my senior, he was like, "Onwukamike Kelechukwu Nnabuike, passed in 5 subjects: Chemistry A, Biology A, Further Mathematics A, Pure

Mathematics A, Physics C with an overall score was 23/25 poi…I did not allow him to finish his sentence before cutting to ask, "Was I the best in the school?" "Yes," he replied and then began to shower me with praise. Petty me, I know, but can you blame me? With all the "you cannot" challenge I was told about GBHS Kumbo, the show off came natural, *lol*. And again the "kill fowl, kill goat" promises my parents made for achieving 1st position. It was a war for me and I could not imagine loosing.

"You have made me so proud," my senior continued. It turned out that he had skipped the first names while searching for my name till he got to the last names. He worried and wondered if I had failed as he could not find mine. Then as he explained later, something prompted him to check the first page, and to his utter shock, my name was enlisted as first. This explained why he delayed calling me back.

I immediately ran to tell my mum. She was beyond excited but insisted we remain calm to avoid creating panic for the others who took the exam and were yet to see their result. Later that afternoon, we celebrated fully on learning that all my study mates passed exceptionally. Then again, I bought the National Daily's newspaper, which published the names of all successful candidates.

The sight of my name as a first-place student from my school and among the top in my region was huge and humbling for me, my friends and family. My former school celebrated my exceptional performance, citing that they provided me with the necessary foundation training. The Nigerian community in the area also celebrated me since this was the first time a Nigerian achieved such.

Contrary to what my senior friend told me, I did not get "lost" but instead made history. Then again I wondered if it would have been so if he did not challenge me in the manner he did. Hence I became thankful to him for indirectly pushing me to go beyond the limits I would have ordinarily avoided.

Moral of my story: When we find ourselves in a new and challenging environment, we can choose to define things for ourselves rather than stay discouraged or afraid by what we were told. You either believe as told or pursue to write your own story. I am a big fan of healthy competitions, especially those that force me out of my comfort zone into a better me.

Like I always say, I now know better how to handle the "you cannot" challenge. If you wish to keep rising to the top, it is important to be careful and watchful about competitions. By all means, avoid pride or jealousy which mostly propels people into unhealthy competitions. There will always be someone ahead of us at all points in our lives, and it does not translate to how their position might relate to who we are, but rather how we can learn from them to improve ourselves. Collaborating and networking are necessary skills that allow us to build sustainable relationships with people more experienced or better in a given area than ourselves, so we cannot take it for granted or overlook it. We must also learn to focus on improving ourselves in the new environment for ourselves first, then for others and the society at large.

4
Impossible Says I'm Possible: My Undergraduate Experience at FUTO

He took a look at my GCE A-level results and asked excitedly, "Wow, this is such an impressive result, which course were you offered?" Industrial Chemistry, I replied with a smile. Oh no! The Chemistry department here is a sad tale. Save yourself the worry of hard-work if your intention is to replicate your excellent GCE A-level results. Just *jejely* (calmly) focus on graduating within the stipulated time. With a melancholy look on his face, he continued, "I am currently in my second year, but within my first year, I and some other students had enrolled in some courses from the Chemistry department. It was terrible in the end as most of us failed."

This conversation was with a random student I met while waiting for my clearance in front of the Senate building in 2008. Thus it felt like God strategically placed people to challenge me in this manner each time I took a new turn in my academic pursuit. Because the timings were just too similar to be a coincidence.

Following my admission into the university, my first task was to validate my results. This exercise was to be carried out at

The Charge

the Senate building. The day I commenced the process, I met the Deputy Vice-Chancellor Academics, who was in charge of the admission clearance process. He referred me to the HOD (Head of Department) Chemistry since I presented a GCE A-level result from Cameroon for a "direct entry admission" instead of the Nigerian Polytechnic OND result.

Since I was now in Nigeria, it was challenging to validate my Cameroonian result.

It happened that the HOD Chemistry was the authority to decide if I would resume as a direct entry student or outright deny me the admission. Resuming as direct entry meant I would join from second-year. I was beyond anxious about his decision as I walked down to his office. My head was spinning; I had millions of internal dialogues. I prayed in my mind all through, asking God to grant me the grace needed to get a positive response from the HOD. Unfortunately, he was not in and I was asked to return the next day.

With time the tension started to ease as I returned the next day and I went to see him. As God may have it, he gave me a yes to direct entry. He further explained that his decision was based on his careful assessment of my past results. This made me extremely happy.

Settling into university life and culture was not the easiest for me. I always had questions to ask about something or somewhere. That's how I came across one nice looking student, nice in terms of friendly because I was careful not to ask anyone. Majority of the students I had met looked stressed and unhappy. So I approached this very one who was "smiling for free" to ask about some departmental course. I assumed he was my level mate that had been in the school longer than I was, but that was not the case. He was instead a Year Four student. Well, I redirected my question to what the journey had been for him. Guess what he said? "the fear of the FUTO Chemistry department is the beginning of wisdom." No department student had graduated with a first-class in the past five years, with only a few since inception. The assertion of this fourth-year Chemistry student further confirmed what I was told earlier by the student I had met during my clearance at the senate. To add more credence to this, I came across the second-year level students results. Their best student was closing out with a CGPA of about 4.2/5.0, which is not bad, by the way, but could be better.

When I finally finished all my registration procedures and resumed classes, the semester exam was near. I resumed classes in January 2008 for a semester that commenced in November 2007; I managed anyway. In no time, I progressed to the third year, and things were no longer strange at this time. I was beginning to enjoy the school and the Chemistry course.

One afternoon in my third year first semester, I was called to the office of our course advisor.

What could this be? What did I do?

I kept asking myself thousands of questions until I recalled that our first semester results had been released. The norm then was to come with a book to write down your grades for the different modules as the course advisor called them out. Checking my results was the only reason I thought warranted the call. When I got to her office, she called out my grades while I noted them in a book. It did not make sense until I

The Charge

finished writing and realised how outstanding my results were. In summary, my CGPA was at 4.44/5.0.

Remember, I was told the Chemistry department was the most arduous ever and many students struggled to make good results. Please take a moment to imagine the joy I felt seeing my result. I was beyond grateful to have made such grades. No wonder I was called because, typically, the students would go themselves. Moving on, my amiable course advisor congratulated me and advised me to work even harder to get the first-class.

In no time, the news of my result had everyone talking; I became an instant celebrity in my department. Most students started getting close to me to find out how I did it. The attention became overwhelming eventually because I was naturally an introverted person.

About a week later, the second-semester results were released. This time, it got even better as I made straight A's in nearly all courses landing my CGPA at 4.56/5.0. It was the best news ever, and I was officially a first-class student. Oh, how happy I was.

All glory to the Most High God, greater are His works indeed. "Except the LORD build the house, they labour in vain that build it: except the LORD keep the city, the watchman waketh but in vain: except the Lord help Kelechukwu, all of his hard and smart work are but in vain." This was my prayer of thanksgiving.

The second-semester news spread even further than the previous one. I became a well-known face among my peers from other departments in the School of Science. I became "that Chemistry student in first-class."

Though I ranked first class from my second year, it was not unusual as most promising students in Chemistry maintained a first-class CGPA upto their third year. After that, things became more challenging due to the increasing complexity of the department core courses that everyone had to take. As a matter of fact, most of these luminous students got into their final year with a CGPA just below 4.5.

The challenge was the part where they had to maintain straight A's with no B in the final year to make a first-class result. Which was in no way a child's play. It was indeed survival of the fittest, and if I for any reason intended to graduate with a first-class, I had to maintain most A's for the rest of the semesters. *"See me, see book, see me, see sleepless nights."* This became my lifestyle.

Despite all the fanfare and attention that came with my exceptional performance, what I appreciated and loved the most was my ability to stay humble. I made a conscious effort always to remind myself why I was enrolled in the university. This clarity helped me to remain calm and collected throughout my study period. The popularity did not get to distract me from the goal. Again my love for Chemistry made it much easier to aim higher than expected. Beyond the first-class dream was a student willing and ready to learn all that was learnable about my course.

The remaining two years were more challenging, coupled with my venturing into campus politics. As a result, I had too many things to manage simultaneously and honestly cannot say how

I got through it all. However, I know that I gave my utmost best on all sides.

Ultimately, I graduated with first-class honours with a CGPA: 4.64/5.0 and was pronounced as the best student from the Chemistry department, the best student from the School of Sciences, and among the top five of the best graduating students of the entire university.

I had called my brother to share the excellent news, and he placed the call on a loudspeaker as he was with Mom and Dad. I heard my mother screaming and shouting for joy. My dad kept clapping his hands and shouting, "that's my boy." It was the best feeling ever. My classmates were ecstatic. It was a grand win for my set as they would be remembered as the set that produced a first-class student in the Chemistry department within the period.

In 2018, seven years after I graduated, another student graduated with a first-class from the Chemistry department. Two others repeated similar feat in 2019 and 2021 respectively. What we were told about the Chemistry department became invalidated through grace, hard-work and determination. Yes, it didn't matter anymore. Instead, what mattered became how to show and guide others towards achieving similar feat.

When one does not create room for "I cannot", they invariably block all the energy intended to put them down. Remember the law of attraction? You are what you think you are. You are what you manifest. Your thoughts become a reality; therefore, never declare the word "impossible" in your vocabulary and life.

Again, who are you listening to? Are you selective about what you feed your mind with? Who are you learning from? Who are your affiliates?

My father often says, "bad company corrupts good character." This phrase hits home; it's easier to get motivated or demotivated owing to the influence we directly or indirectly surround ourselves.

I honestly aim to live a fulfilled life, and in my bid to do so, I avoid arguments to disprove those who doubt or place a limitation on my capability. What I do is work and put in my best, and I do it for me because I believe I can, and that's the I'm possible mindset.

No mountain is too high to climb, so when someone tells you something is impossible, say to them: "I'm possible," because honestly, you can achieve what you set your mind to achieve. Also, do not live your life because you want to prove someone wrong; you don't have to. The goal is to achieve it for yourself; trust me, it rubs off on everyone around you *las las* (lastly).

If you have to leave your comfort zone, leave it, look yourself in the mirror each time you are faced with any challenge and remind yourself that you can, and it is possible.

5

Tell My Teacher: He Made Me Careful to Succeed

First, it was a relative, then an older friend, followed by a stranger with a senior student at the university and now? This story will tell. The point is, we are inescapably surrounded by people who, for different reasons, can challenge our capabilities. I am sure it would be a lot easier on us if we had a way to influence how they communicate their thoughts to us, but unfortunately, we can't control this. Just know that, people will always talk. In most cases, the intention behind the talks is not to demean or discourage us. Irrespective of the reasons, it is important that we don't allow these talks to become our problem. I understand it can be pretty challenging to overlook, but what would the worry or feeling of dissuasion fetch? Nothing.

Here is to answer the question & feedback from my LinkedIn network after my post on "Tell my teacher" went viral on social media. Sometime last year, I shared an experience with my teacher from High School days. This teacher had presumed the outcome of my result in a bid to advise me.

This happened in May 2007, during my high school days and during my GCE A-level Chemistry practical examination. I had looked up to take a deep breath but immediately, noticed that my chemistry teacher whom I once told I would make a A-grade in chemistry, was watching me. I recall making the statement from a place of faith and over a normal conversation in the past. He was seriously staring at me and I could not understand why. I guess he noticed how uncomfortable I became and so he walked up to my table. There were many other students in the laboratory, so I wondered why he had chosen to come to my own work space. He then came closer and whispered into my ears;

"Is this how you are going to make an A-grade in Chemistry?"

E shock me! (I was shocked) and immediately, I became unsettled and stood akimbo like someone lost in the middle of no where. I took some steps back to recheck my work many times but could not identify what I did or was doing wrong in my experiment. Sincerely speaking, I struggled to finish. He continued monitoring me, and it made it even harder to concentrate. In the end, I barely completed recording my last experiments results before the stipulated time was over.

With so many thoughts running through my mind, I made my way out of the laboratory. Towards the exit door, I met him again. This time, he had even more distressing things to say. According to him, I had done too many things wrong in my experiment and with what he saw, the A-grade I told him I would make in Chemistry will not happen.

His feedback ruined my entire day. Nonetheless, I found a way to comfort myself with the upcoming sections of the Chemistry examination. As always, I gave my best in the remaining papers of the Chemistry exam and left the rest.

Two months later, the final results were released. Only two people out of the entire class made an A-grade in the said Chemistry course, and surprisingly, I was one out of the two. Saying I was overjoyed would be an understatement. I was beyond happy to see my result. Somehow, I did not accommodate any hard feelings for my teacher or remember what he said about my result earlier.

One afternoon while in school to collect my statement of result, we ran into each other. After exchanging pleasantries, I joyfully announced my result to him. What was said and not said did not matter anymore, as success was at the centre of the entire conversation. He smiled and congratulated me. Whether or not he meant it did not also matter, I wholeheartedly accepted it, and we went our separate ways afterwards.

Fast forward to what you already know, I continued my journey with Chemistry at the University, completed my bachelor with first-class honours. To cut the long story short, in February 2019, I defended my double PhD in Chemistry. The viral post on blogs coined it as "12 years after." It was indeed twelve years after. However, I achieved this because I stayed true to giving my best to what I loved and wanted.

Provided you don't quit, and not willing to stay on the floor after falling: what the next person says is secondary. The top decision-maker is yourself.

While I cannot complete my success story without the immense contribution of my teachers at various phases of my life, I also chose not to ignore those whose approaches were not the most supportive. Like I said earlier, their intentions may be right but might not come out right. Exactly why it should not be the focus. So, until tomorrow, the focus, decision, and choices are on you.

Let me bring to your attention the words of one of the most famous inventors of the 19th century, Henry Ford: "If you think you can, you are correct; if you think you can't, you are correct." In my words, you can choose your own "correct."

6
Is Education a Scam?

Hmmm, what do you think?
I do agree that not everyone will fulfil their purpose through education. Nonetheless, it would always be a significant 'add-on' for secondary users as such.

Primarily, for people like myself who love education and will choose it over and again as a gateway to fulfilling purpose, we cannot help but preach how tremendously it has helped us grow and succeed. If you had the opportunity to read the preceding stories, you would understand me when I say education brought out the best in me.

Most of the times I got challenged to become better, it was because of school. From my cousin, "on the first position" when I was just a little boy to my older friend from my high school. Then the stranger and senior student at university followed by my teacher, and the list continues. It may have been different if the environment was different, say I was helping my parents hawk plantain chips. Then I would most likely be writing about how I met an uncle who challenged me to sell more plantain or a senior person in the business who made me apply more business acumen.

The reason some people may perceive education as a scam is hinged on surrounding realities, and it's difficult to blame them. I'll tell you why.

A few years ago in Nigeria, the video of a young boy of about 12-14 years of age trended on social media platforms. In the video, the boy gave a blunt response after being asked why he wasn't in school. He vehemently told the interviewer that going to school amounted to nothing, and he had evidence to support his statement. Firstly, his experience with the graduates he knew personally and those living within his environment. In his words, many of them were still eating *"Mama, Thank You"*. Meaning they were unemployed and still depended on their parents for food and livelihood. The same parents who spent time and resources to send them to school still made to cater even after graduation.

Sad, right? It simply doesn't add up.

As a child, I remember the many instances I watched my mother pray to God to bless her children with befitting jobs upon graduation, which is pretty much the prayer of many parents. It's a reward deserving of parents that a child they trained through school become successful citizens in the community, country and world at large. But in situations where graduates roam the streets with no jobs, hence no source of livelihood except their parents, how then are the other parents encouraged to send their wards to school?

The Charge

How do you also convince the 12-year-old boy and other children that the future is bright?

How do you make meaning of the narrative that going to school is neither a scam nor a waste of time?

How, please?

The little boy did not only hear education failed graduates, he saw for himself. He probably had big dreams, but with such experience, education was not the best route to actualize those aspirations. Can we blame him?

When his video went viral, it sparked serious conversations and controversy about the decadence in the country's educational system, yet not much has changed of late.

Take another example whereby 2021 top-achieving graduate students from different departments at the University of Nigeria, Nsukka, were awarded a cash prize of ₦1,500 ($3) each. Same as I was given ten years ago when I emerged the best graduating student from my department and the entire Faculty of Sciences. I'll save the details of what transpired when I went to claim the award and cash prize for another day. Just know that to date, I have not received any of the things that was promised.

Surprisingly, the same country where top-achieving graduates are rewarded $3 is the same country where reality television winners are appointed and awarded millions of naira by the system in addition to their reward from the show producers. Please don't twist my words; I have no problems with reality television shows. But really, where do our priorities lie?

Barack Obama, in one of his speeches, said:

"In the 21st century, the best anti-poverty program around is a world-class education."

Do we all see with his lenses?

Does our country share the same sentiments?

And I ask again, can we blame the boy?

Sometime this year, I reached out to my academic mentor in Nigeria, a professor *per* excellence who was awarded the best Natural Scientist in Nigeria and among the top 2% globally in his field.

I was pretty concerned about the welfare of students and was curious to learn some things that bothered me about them, especially how they strived to study despite the staggering double-digit unemployment statistics and other discouraging issues in the country. Because truthfully speaking, Nigerian youths love to get educated regardless. In my case, I did it out of love and determination to give my current and future family a better life than I had. The thought alone kept me going against all the odds. And today I am grateful that it did not fail me. So learning about what inspires others stuck on my mind till I asked my Professor the following questions.

"Prof, what do you think motivates your students to keep studying?"

"What assures them of a bright future after school?"

He gave me a similar response as my grandmother did whenever we consulted her for advice:

"Do not allow your circumstances define your endeavours or future."

The Charge

Whether or not his response was the real motivation for his students, one thing was clear: many still believed in the power education has to transform a person.

For this singular belief, I chose to mentor and inspire them; the 12 year old and others alike in my little way. Via my mentorship platform: DEKEMP; story telling, *Till We All Win book;* summits: Global Scholarship summits and other avenues and outreach events.

Considering the reality within the shores of our county, these activities do not come cheap or easy on me, notwithstanding the thought of giving hope to graduate students keeps me going.

Provided you know and believe in the significance of education, I urge you to light up another candle. You may not have arrived as we remain a work in progress. However, there is no perfect timing to change a life. Do well to encourage yourself, your neighbour, and those within and outside your reach that the grass is greener on the other side. Become that motivation.

In my case, my older brother was. He inspired me to keep up my faith and work harder. A few months after graduation, I watched him land a prominent job at Procter & Gamble Nigeria. In a short while, he won the prestigious Erasmus Mundus Scholarship worth over forty thousand euros (€40,000) in 2008. The scholarship afforded him a world-class education/training that our parents would naturally not have been able to afford. His love and die-hard spirit for education rubbed off nicely on me. Though I also loved education, I saw my future in his present. And it was so bright I was willing to do the most to succeed.

Watching and learning from my older brother and other supportive people around helped me reach outstanding career goals upon graduation.

Growing up, we were neither rich nor poor, so I can easily relate to some struggles. My parents did their best in laying a good educational background for us, and by the special Grace of God, it was good enough. Today, I am a product of quality education, and my journey demonstrates how a nobody can become somebody, literally.

Between the inception of my MSc, to the completion of my PhD studies, I received over three hundred and fifty thousand euros (€350,000), equivalent to 200 million naira in scholarships. In addition, the golden opportunity to research in state-of-the-art laboratories in Europe and attend international conferences throughout Europe and the USA. There is no way my parents could have afforded such expensive postgraduate programmes, *Lai Lai!* (not possible).

No wonder, during one of my visits to Nigeria, my dad so proudly introduced me to his peers as "the youngest PhD holder around", and one of them replied that "education is indeed the route through which the child of anyone can become someone." Didn't I say it before now?

As I look once more at the story of the 12-year-old boy, I sincerely wish I could meet him and share my story. But, more so, to many who may have lost faith in education, I would love for them to learn from me: my mistakes, my resilience, my loss, and my wins.

Maybe you are the one who asked about my motivation to mentor students; well, you have just arrived at the answer. Dr

KC Mentorship platform (DEKEMP) was born from a passion to inspire undergraduate/graduate students and give hope to as many that need it. Assuring them that education, no matter what, is rewarding.

My joy within the short time (3 years) since DEKEMP was founded are the many lives that have been changed for good. Over one hundred and thirty-five DEKEMP scholars have received international scholarships valued at over seven million five hundred thousand US dollars ($7,500,000) in developed world countries such as the USA, United Kingdom, Europe, and Asia. The fact that my guidance helped them achieve this feats is beyond magical for me. It is fulfilling.

Again, through the collective effort of other scholarship awardees and platforms such as mine, the First-Class Leaders Network, Erasmus Mundus Nigeria Group, Dr Michael Taiwo Scholarships, i-Scholar Initiative, Education USA, over one hundred Nigerian graduates in 2021 alone received the Erasmus Mundus Scholarship worth fifty thousand Euros (€50,000) per awardee. Another fifty Nigerians were selected for the Chevening Scholarship in the United Kingdom plus the Commonwealth Shared scholarship that hundreds of Nigerians got in 2021.

As my brother would say, "you can't teach people about something you've never learned nor experienced." I concur with his words because what I have given to my mentees and still giving is my experience in black and white. "Till we all win" is therefore, a photocopy of my life journey. The other platforms I mentioned earlier have also done similar things with the same types of results. Hence it takes one to lift another, and we cannot undermine the impact of real-life stories and mentors.

In Oprah Winfrey's words, "education is the key to unlocking the world and a passport to freedom."

Education is aimed to empower us to become productive and prolific in our society.

Education is meant to change lives for the better and transform mental and intellectual capacities.

If someone like me managed to get this far through education, I genuinely believe many others can.

Beyond the monetary values of international scholarships, the opportunity to gain world-class education is golden. It unravels the very best of us to create, build, resolve, restore, heal, and the list continues.

Be it home or abroad, the significance of quality education cannot be overemphasized.

If you or someone you know had doubts on the benefit of education, I hope my story and that of many who have succeeded through this path has helped in addressing this.

Education is a win-win and never a scam.

THEME 2:
Beyond Physical Appearance

7
Worth More than Our Looks: Someone Like Me

"Why don't you come and join Nollywood? I bet you'll make a really good kisser in the movies." Said the movie producer whom I approached at Enugu, to market my movie scripts. This was me in 2009 exploring newer means of earning in order to support my educational needs. Since I had been writing for fun in the past, I reasoned that Nollywood script writing would be lucrative. In my assay, it was going to be easy and fun, no stress at all. So I began writing scripts. On the very day I got the "kissing role" reply, I was out to sell one of my scripts to a movie producer on set. The nerve of me. So after my long sermon on the wonder story I had written, he offered me the opportunity to take a kissing role in the movie they were shooting.

The first thought that came to mind was my parents and it was enough to decline the tempting offer. So I immediately replied, "thank you but no Sir, I'll rather you buy my scripts, they are really nice."

But then he insisted that, he couldn't do beyond the offer he gave me. Besides I had nothing to back my self acclaimed script writing skills compared to the kissing that I would easily carry out: based on my swagged-up look and fine face.

Ha! I screamed and we burst out laughing. Post that, we engaged in a more serious conversation. He was quite shocked to learn I was in my 3rd year and when I added that I was already a first class student, he struggled to believe it. To him I appeared more like an unserious play boy, the reason he offered the kissing role in the first place. In any case he felt bad that he judged me wrongly. This encounter was just one of the many instances where my potential was judged on how I looked or dressed.

For example, in my first year at the university: Within the first few days of resumption, one of my classmates got very close to me, we bonded pretty well and became good friends in a short while. We became so close that going everywhere and anywhere together became a norm. Unknown to us, our friendship was annoying some people to the extent he got called out by one of his friends who wanted to understand why he was moving too close to someone like me. According to the friend, I dressed and looked very unserious all the time and he could not deal with the fact that I was definitely going to influence him in a bad way. My dear friend in defense began to explain how contrary his definition of me was. He even charged him with a conviction that I could emerge best student. But no, it made matters worse instead, since our results were yet to be released. The conversation ended sour and my friend returned to tell me.

Question is how did I look and dress? Well, I often wore bright colours, not necessarily because I chose them but because they came in handy from my wardrobe. In other words, I wore what I had and met clean in my *ghana-must-go* sized wardrobe. And my so-called fine boy afro was there because I would save the money for hair cuts to cater for more pressing needs. Only I knew what I was doing, I'm sure he would still not have understood if I explained it to him. so I simply kept my cool. Within a short period from that time, our first semester came out and yours sincerely: *Mr fine boy with unserious look* made the best grades. Hallelujah! A week later, the second-semester results followed, and I officially became the only first-class student in my class. It was a big deal because such results were highly uncommon in the department. I could tell because of the amount of work I put in to earn the results. For what it's worth, I needed to try my best to change the *fine boy no brain* narrative. It didn't come easy but it did eventually. All glory to God. On a second note, performance stood out for my friend as he proudly went back my accuser to justify why he was not wrong in choosing me to be his friend despite my dressing style. After this incident, his friend's opinion of me took an entirely new turn, and we eventually became friends.

I'm sure these types of stories are not peculiar to me, as I have witnessed cases where people were quick to attribute the good results of beautiful ladies to being favoured by male lecturers and not due to their hard work.

Beyond Physical Appearance

More broadly, many people are judged based on their skin colour, background, affiliation, tribe, and other reasons, taking away the place of merit and hard work. It's simply unkind as everyone has a right to how they dress and express themselves. When assessing someone for a position, it is imperative to emphasise the required core skills rather than draw conclusions based on looks.

Again, it is an expression of wisdom not to write people off based on physical appearance. Hence we can do better by allowing people showcase themselves as the chances remain high that behind looks could lie a rare gem. Since not everyone is strong enough to manage critics, in calling out an emotionally sensitive person owing to their looks or dressing style, one might be shutting down a generational gift. Let's learn to give people a chance no matter how they look, appear or sound. For we are all worth more than our looks.

8
Respect Open Doors: My Second-Year Internship Experience

"How have you managed to stay respectful despite all your accomplishments?" This was one of the questions my LinkedIn connections wanted me to cover in this book. My response is that being respectful has been a big contributor to the many "doors" that got opened for me. I agree with the famous saying that "the way to the top is from the bottom." A respectful attitude will facilitate your journey to a higher altitude. Therefore, each time I walk out the door, I intentionally remind myself to be respectful and never take anyone for granted. Irrespective of who they are, I am very intentional to be respectful to people I come across.

This respectful attitude of mine came in handy when I looked for internship placement as a second-year undergraduate student.

When it was time to commence my internship, I got back home to request help from my dad since he was very vast with manufacturing companies in my state. He made some recommendations but didn't have any personal contact at these places. So I was then left to go and try my luck.

One of those places was Ebony Paint Nigeria Limited, located in Enugu. I headed to Enugu town the next day with my CV and internship placement form. After asking for directions from road users, I ended up at the company facility. Upon arriving, I saw that everywhere looked deserted. However, it was evident from the structures that this was an important company in the past but not anymore.

I wasn't sure if the company was still operational, so I approached the security man at the gate. "Is this company still functional?" I asked. "Yes," he replied and added, "Oga is in the other building," while pointing to the next building. When I got there, I met three men and a lady. One of the men was hand-mixing paints while the others sat at a distance discoursing.

From a first look, one would imagine that the person hand-mixing the paint couldn't be the boss as this was the most menial job. As I approached them, I bowed in respect and greeted all of them. "I am here to find an internship placement," I said after the greetings. "Why this company?" the man who was hand-mixing the paint asked without looking up. "Because I am interested in learning the practical aspect of producing paint so as to consolidate the theory that I have learnt in school," I replied. The man stopped mixing, cleaned his hands, and asked me to hand over my CV and internship placement form. After looking through it, he nodded his head and said I could start the following week.

Just like that! I was lost for words as I clinched my internship position in my first shot.

When I called my dad that evening, he couldn't believe his ears when I told him I finally got an internship placement. The following week, I started my internship, which was one of the best practical experiences I have ever had. The training allowed me to learn how to produce paints and exposed me to entrepreneurship.

For the record, second-year internships in Nigeria are more challenging to find compared to fourth-year internships. One of the reasons is due to its short duration of 3months, when compared to the fourth year internship that runs for six months. Hence, most industries are unwilling to accept students that will stay for such short durations, considering the time needed for their onboarding.

Despite how difficult getting such an internship placement, I was able to get one on the first try. When I look back to the circumstances that led to securing this internship position, I couldn't be more correct if I accorded my respect to the boss of this company as what gave me an edge. Though I met him for the first time doing the most menial job, I didn't look down on him. When I finally resumed my internship, the boss mentioned that he was very unwilling to receive students for IT placements, despite that many have accosted him over the past year. "Why then did you choose me?" I asked. "You were respectful," he replied.

It is very clear from my experience that we might never know who we meet both online and offline. It is thus imperative that we stay respectful as this will usually win us a place. We shouldn't take anyone for granted because of their appearance,

Beyond Physical Appearance

judging a book by its cover will cost us more than we can ever imagine.

Indeed, respect opens doors.

9
Mother the Situation: Set the Pace

I have always described my kind mother as my number one fan, and that's for many reasons. Fundamentally, she is a jewel in the crown. I mean the best of the best. In wisdom, love and humility, she raised us (my siblings and I) and not once has she stopped to pray that we continue to walk in that same light. In a manner that is hard to overlook, she puts us first and would go all the way to ensure we are cared for, protected and safe.

As much as possible, she avoided engaging in any physical altercation with anyone and taught us to avoid trouble. The escape code was to exchange kindness for the rage and step back in the face of any.

We tried oh, we tried. Nonetheless, I still have some warrior marks on me. Some petty *small pikin* (kids) fights were sadly unavoidable. Not a problem, though, but she should never hear about it else the punishment was sure to hurt more than the blows from such fights. She disliked physical confrontations a lot and disciplined us to avoid them completely. Breaking any societal rule or regulation, on the other hand, was a no-no. We dared not. But this one time, the confrontation came knocking on our doorstep, the time when I got arrested by the police right before her at age thirteen. Story of my life, *huh*.

Though Nigerian by nationality, I was born and raised in Cameroon till age eighteen. Cameroon, I must say, is a lovely country. Nice landscapes, variety of food, fun people, fun-filled Christmas celebrations, sound primary and secondary education system, different languages, including the Cameroon pidgin that is still in use in my family to date. It was "somewhat" home away from home. Christmas was my best time because during this time, there was this custom of visiting friends and neighbours to get c*hin chin* (a common crunchy and tasty fried snack in some parts of Africa).

Amidst all the fantastic recollections of my childhood memories, there were equally unpleasant times and events. We did try to grow over them, but it was not comfortable at the time. Remember I said living in Cameroon was "somewhat" home away from home. The reason for the somewhat is owing to the unpleasant times and events we faced.

For one, the energy we often received within and outside our neighbourhood made us aware of our foreign status. At every point, it reminded us that we were Nigerians and not Cameroonians. My high school Physics teacher, for example, during classes, made it a duty each time he is chanced to outrightly remind me that I was a foreigner in his country. In addition, many Nigerians were called derogatory names that simply communicated to them of their foreign status.

During game periods, especially when Nigeria had a football match with Cameroon, irrespective of where the game was being watched, we were made to conceal any form of excitement, were Nigerians to win the game. When we watched such games at home, my mother would ensure we did not celebrate openly or show any sign of excitement not to upset our Cameroonian neighbours. I may have been a child, but it still didn't feel right to me. I may not have understood it thoroughly, but it was glaring that we did not belong fully to that society. We also had to deal with some immigration issues that didn't add up, making it more glaring that we come second.

Over time, we grew a thick skin until the day of my arrest; this incident tore the skin completely. This was the first and only time I had been arrested, and I was just thirteen.

That very day, I was busy helping my mum at our business premises when some immigration officers, on their routine immigration inspection, stormed into my mother's shop and got me arrested.

They claimed my stay was illegal because I didn't have a Cameroonian residence permit. My mother, in defence, tried in vain to convince them otherwise. She presented my birth certificate, which showed I was born in Cameroon, and my student identity card, which showed I was a student. But they didn't accept any and insisted that she either present my residence permit or they will take me with them. Since I didn't have it, my poor mother gave in and helplessly watched as they whisked me onto their bus that was already half-filled with other arrested Nigerians.

I was taken to the police station, and I remained there for hours until my uncle came, liaised with them, and finalised the conditions for my release. He had to pay for the acclaimed residence permit fee and a fine.

I left the police station feeling so bitter. If it were possible to disappear and appear in Nigeria, I would have done it. I didn't want anything to do with Cameroon anymore. For heaven's sake, I was thirteen, and this was in Africa.

"My continent!" I murmured.

I was heartbroken, not necessary because of the arrest but the fact that it happened right before my mother. Within that period, it wasn't easy to relate properly with Cameroonians. However, the pain was not going to last forever, so my family and I moved past it with time.

In addition, since the arrest event happened during school holidays, it was easier to close the chapter before school reopened. But then again, another drama welcomed me back to school.

It was in my Form five class at PCHS Kumbo. We had written our mock exam before the holidays, and right after we resumed, the results were released. I got hold of mine and was filled with excitement because I had passed with distinction. I looked around the class in my moment of joy, hoping to rejoice with others but realised I was the only one smiling. It turned out that I was the only one who made an A-grade while over 90% of the class failed. I was the only Nigerian in class with the rest, Cameroonians. As usual, I concealed my excitement. It was natural to do so, courtesy of my mother. But at that same moment, I began to ponder.

For how long was this attitude of concealing victory going to continue, and why should I care? It's not like they love and accept me fully per se. I should be rejoicing to spite them. Some payback spite for my arrest by their police, at least.

"Is not happening", I said after the wild thinking.

Within the following minutes, my heart was filled with empathy again, and this time I began to reason how I was going to help my classmates. I wanted them to succeed like me, and it didn't matter who they were or what I felt they represented. I just wanted to help, and for the very first time, I came up with the idea of tutorials as a means of achieving a collective win. I reapplied this approach in my high school which led to creating a study group that achieved 100% pass at the Advanced level GCE as shared in the previous chapter. But it is worth remembering how this mindset started and eventually gave birth to my "till we all win" ideology. And over the years, I kept fine-tuning its execution to what you know today as DEKEMP. I have expanded this experience and how it transformed my mindset to start working towards a "collective win" in a later chapter of this book.

But just like you, dear reader, repaying unfairness with kindness is not as easy as it sounds. Forget motivational speaking. It's a conscious effort. Remove my mother from my childhood, and you would have a different man. But for her discipline and exemplary character, I would not be here encouraging you to be the kinder one. Being ill-treated by people we call brothers and sisters, sadly, have come to stay. From experience, I can tell that it hurts badly. Yet, I encourage you to exchange it for kindness like my mother.

Beyond Physical Appearance

The truth is, there will always be that person or people threatened by your existence, so bad they want to rub it on your face. But it will only happen if you allow them to get to you. No matter where you are now or where you go tomorrow, you will somehow find them but guess what? The change they need to experience is your kindness. Yes, you can mother the situation and in this way set the pace.

9.1 Mr "Your Fahrkarte"

"Talk about being treated differently by people who look like you" was my thought when I encountered the person I have now code-named Mr "Your Fahrkarte."

The time was past 7:00 pm, I had closed later than usual from work, and all that mattered was how fast I could get home. As I walked to the bus station, being one of those cold winter evenings, I prayed silently that the bus shouldn't be delayed. "Thank God," I said to myself when I saw the bus approaching on time. When the bus came to a stop, I peeped through the driver window and saw that the driver looked like me, a black man; a feeling of camaraderie engulfed me like it does most of the time when I meet people that looked like me abroad.

Waiting with me at the bus station were two people; I was the only black person in their midst. So when the bus stopped, I walked past the driver and went to my seat just like the two people before me.

I was about to stretch my legs when the driver called out to me. I looked around to be sure I was the one, and he insisted it was me. Since I was the only black person, it was undeniably obvious what was unfolding before my eyes, and I guess in the eyes of the other commuters. I stood to find out why and he immediately muttered: *Dein Fahrkarte?* (German language which translates to "your bus ticket?"). In my state of mixed emotions, I gently presented my ticket and walked back to my seat. It took a few steps, but then it felt like miles. It was outright embarrassing for me.

Throughout that trip, my mind kept analysing the incidence. Should I call him out? What should I say to him? Why would he single me out of the rest? Like why?

No idea made sense, so I just kept my cool, and I alighted at my stop. It was just too difficult to process the experience. The driver was a black man just like me, and it just felt like he used me to prove his diligence. But why didn't he request the other two passengers to show their tickets? I couldn't find an answer.

Each time I recall the experience, I regret not asking him why.

As I went home that evening, I kept asking myself what would my mother do? "treat people with kindness, even when they are underserving" she will say. These words soothe my heart and perhaps acted as an immune booster to such discrimination. I consider that being able to mother the situation doesn't help me alone but also the perpetrators. My reason for thinking in this direction is that I might be the healing they need. We all cannot be sick, you know, someone has to play the doctor role.

Every passing day, we hear stories about people treating other people unfairly—all shades of discrimination polluting our environment like CO_2 daily. Overtime, I realised that I honestly didn't give it much attention anymore. Some of my friends call this approach of dealing with discrimination, "immunity," which even makes it hard to pick on subtle or outright discrimination. However, my supposed immunity does not in any way undermine the experiences of others. On the contrary, I respect other people's experiences for sure.

In instances when my immunity fails like it did with my Mr "Your Fahrkarte" encounter, I find myself asking the question, "how would my mother respond?" It is a self-reflective question that helps me draw from my mother's kindness-full upbringing. And it is from this kindness I find a way to address such experiences.

Since kindness enabled me to go through such difficult experiences, I would share how colourful kindness can help beautify our world.

10

Kindness is Colourful

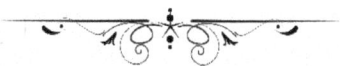

Kindness is colourful. Treating others the way they would love to be treated is well-rooted in Jesus's response to the question, "what is the greatest commandment? Which was, "love your neighbour as you love yourself" (Matthew 22:37-39). Do you love yourself? How do you show love to yourself? Being able to express that to others is the most prominent judge of our personality. As seen in the previous chapter, discrimination can be seen as the lowest of any form of human interaction. I have been shown kindness on many occasions by strangers who had little or nothing to gain from helping me. As a person, I am very conscious of how I treat people, thanks to my mother and an expression of that kindness can be seen in a few examples that I will share in the following paragraphs.

Sometime in 2019, I got a message from a connection on LinkedIn. He had just gotten a scholarship for a dual MSc programme in France and Germany but was stuck in Nigeria because he couldn't afford his flight ticket. My first response was to advise him to reach out to his immediate circle of

Beyond Physical Appearance

friends and family to raise the money. After about two weeks, I reached out to him for an update. Not only was he not able to still raise this money, but his admission was also already at risk as his program was already almost two months gone. If he failed to make it to France within a week, he would lose a grant worth millions of naira. I reached out to my LinkedIn network and solicited support on his behalf without hesitation. The responses were massive, and within 24h the target was not only achieved but surpassed. From standing on the verge of losing such a prestigious offer to being in France within two days looked like a dream to him. To add a cherry to the cake, in 2021, being two years after I helped him get his flight ticket sorted out, he got a prestigious full PhD funding at one of Europe's elite universities, TU Deft Netherlands! In my consideration to offer assistance to this connection, who became my mentee, I never factored in the fact that he did not share the same religion as me, nor did we come from the same ethnicity and geographical location in Nigeria. At this point, he wasn't even part of my mentorship platform, DEKEMP. However, what mattered then and now was that a brilliant guy was about to lose a prestigious offer/dream. Therefore I had to step in.

In another instance, my mentee got accepted into the NAWA scholarship in 2020. Once more, he couldn't afford the associated cost of his flight to Poland. Having been his mentor for a while and understood his background, I knew something had to be done fast. Time was quickly running out after he explored all the available resources around him to no avail. I reached out to my LinkedIn connection to solicit help on his behalf. The response was again massive, and within 48h the target was not only reached but surpassed. The other missing piece was getting from Zamfara to Lagos for his departing flight. Having never been to Lagos, I reached out to my mentees in Lagos to get their support. Many of them offered to accommodate him for the night before his flight. Finally, one of them offered to make himself available to pick him from the bus station, house him for the night and equally take him to the airport. This is precisely how it played out, and this mentee of mine was able to join the other scholars in Poland. Nothing was important to me in my quest to support this mentee than the fact that we are all humans irrespective of religion, ethnicity and background. In 2021, I successfully sought financial support through my LinkedIn connections towards flight fare for three of my mentees that faced similar constraints. These mentees are currently in the USA and Thailand.

Kindness is indeed so colourful. Nothing beats the sincere and warm smile we can give and receive with people we meet on the streets or that inner joy knowing that your actions have just kept the hope of someone alive.

We are all unique; no two people have the same DNA, which is evidence of our uniqueness. This uniqueness shouldn't be a basis of segregation but rather a huge potential. Our diversity brings colour to this world. From my perspective, the foundation of a just society is hinged on us recognising the potential of diversity as a bridge rather than a wall. The question that keeps running through my mind is, "can we will ever live in a world where we are not judged by the colour of our skin, ethnicity and belief, but by the content of our character?" My answer to this question is a *yes*, but this will only be possible when we start treating others with kindness and no prejudice. To move the world, we have to start by

Beyond Physical Appearance

moving ourselves. To have a kind society, we have to start by showing kindness, and this ripple effect gradually spreads to our society and the world at large. Let our first response to a stranger not be one of suspicion but one of openness where we recognise that we don't know what we don't know but are always willing to learn. Kindness is so colourful that we don't have to show it as a form of reciprocating but as something beautiful that naturally flows from within ourselves towards others. We can choose to be kind irrespective of how we are being treated. The golden rule of kindness remains that "we treat others how they would love to be treated."

THEME 3:
Work In Progress

11
No One's Head is Touching the Ceiling

The year was 2007, and I was in High school, Upper-Sixth Science class. During this time, I was privileged to be under the tutorship of a great man, my Further Maths teacher. Beyond $X+Y=0$, he taught me practical lessons about life, some of which I have carried on to date. One memory of him that I have kept with me is the title of this chapter "no one's head is touching the ceiling."

It was a sunny afternoon, and we were quietly seated in his class. No one had the time or energy to discuss anything else rather than the task at hand. Usually, when assigned homework, we'd return to class to learn the answers, that is, after we must have submitted it to our teacher. The exercise was always quick and enlightening, but the story was different on this very occasion. A particular question kept everyone on the spot longer than expected. Everyone tried what they knew, but nothing worked. Finally, out of frustration, one of my classmates stood up and spoke the mind of the entire class to our teacher.

"Sir, we cannot do this, it's simply unsolvable. Would you please give us the solution?"

In response, my teacher looked up and down the ceiling and then asked

"Class, do you see any head up the ceiling?"

No, we replied but wondered why he asked such a question.

He then went further to reply: the reason you cannot see anyone´s head up the ceiling is that no one's head is touching the ceiling. As it were, "all heads in this class, including mine, is below the roof."

He explained how impractical it was for us to think he knew all the answers simply because he was our teacher. Then, moving on, he asked that we all work together as a team with him inclusive to get the solution.

Within the following minutes, everyone froze. No way!

He could have asked us to take it home again and rework it or something else but not openly confess that he could also not solve the problem just like us.

Now different people will read different meanings to the event, but for us that day, it was the most shocking and humbling experience. Personally, my respect for him doubled. He was one of the most brilliant teachers I knew, and for him to admit to not knowing everything to the whole class? That was wow!

In explaining this concept, let us look at what "ceiling" means using basic economics. In the context of price-fixing, the government can impose what they call "ceiling price," which forces everyone not to sell above a given price. This decision ensures that essential commodities do not get so expensive that the local population cannot afford them.

How does this explanation apply to a learner? There is simply no "learner ceiling" enforced by a government or society as to how much we can learn. A learner does not embark on the journey of self-discovery and fulfilment with the intention that there is a "ceiling" to which his head will touch and thus be considered as one who has "arrived." Therefore, a wise learner, as my teacher for example, continues to learn, recognising that there is always something new to learn. This mindset opens the mind to new possibilities and humbles the human ego.

The lifelong learner mindset also makes meaning of the "we are all a work in progress" philosophy.

Coming to terms that no one knows it all, has it all figured out or owns it all, opens new opportunities to progress in our different life works. How much more when we choose to work in synergy, which would make our world an even better place.

12
The Road Travelled

I find it very interesting to learn how the vast majority of us have gained mastery in advertising success. Almost every post on social media elevates success, be it personal or related. And frankly speaking, success is worth the attention, so why not. It's only natural to share the good news. Through back-to-back success posts and stories, we can all agree that many influencers have arisen. Almost exceeding the number of people that are being influenced, and often, you would notice that in a bid to keep up with traffic on a page, people post wins regardless of whether or not they are genuinely succeeding.

Like I earlier said, it is only natural and beautiful to share wins, awards, and achievements on social media. Amazing culture! But then, it would also be nice to harmonise it with the typical struggles that fed, sheltered, and clothed such wins. The impulse is thus to read and learn rather than read, admire and wish. If you can already relate to what I mean, I urge you to do it differently. I'm so looking forward to times when we can start to include the fated hurdles and turbulence we faced on board our journey to success. In my opinion, this will make the stories more human and enlivening. In this regard, a sneak peek into what goes down before the crown would be nice to read, thus providing the reader an opportunity to learn through the process you went through. I mean, it would be refreshing to come online and see some unkept hairs, puzzled faces, rumpled shirts or is the success that ironed out? I don't believe so, because success is churned out from repeated failure.

I think we have done the usual long enough, and it's about time we start to commonise the processes alongside the struggle *as e dey* hot (as soon as possible). Imagine a post that reads:

"Hello, LinkedIn Fam, I just failed my job interview." or

"Dear LinkedIn family, my hundredth scholarship application returned negative."

No, it is not promoting failure because if we look much deeper, it is relatively too clear to ignore that the majority of people that will come by the post will relate to it naturally. Some, such as myself, will not look past without leaving a comment or two. And the first comment would be to applaud the author for owning the struggle. And second, would be to chip in some morale-booster for the author to make the hundred and one application the next day. Having hopes that the narrative would start to change, I would expect that other commenters offer other forms of assistance to right whatever was done wrongly or poorly. In the end, championing the author to go harder and better.

As a mentor, hearing people complain about not doing enough or running behind goals is very common. But it's not always easy for me to fully digest. So, I typically would ask to learn about the reference point for the lateness. And the majority of the time, it boils down to what other classmates, colleagues, and the rest of the world is achieving and posting. In other words, the frequency of successful posts on their peer's social media page compared to theirs is the reason why they feel they are late or not doing enough. In my opinion, it should not be so because behind the many successful posts lies the constantly striving individual, just like the reader who is also pushing to succeed. In addition, underneath these posts lies dozens of failures, sleepless nights, restlessness and so on. But because they are mostly undisclosed, it has unintentionally made it difficult to believe that, indeed, hard work is the achiever's framework. And by hiding them, a random motivational post about success appears foreign and is almost always followed by an undertone of jest about the author. Who is wrongly understood to have created fictitious stories of their past for likes, shares, and retweets. On one hand is the one making posts and on the other, the striving reader who, trying not to be seen as unsuccessful and as a result, more likely to follow the route of "fake it till you make it." Who then is deceiving who and to what end? We have a generation to inspire, and the goal should be to do it right.

I'd love to share a practical example to drive home this message. And it's about my encounter with a retired headmaster during my service year. He was supposed to be my landlord, but he went beyond that to mentor me through the entire year I spent in his housing property. We became friends not long after I moved in. We talked almost every week, and each time, I had a lesson to take home.

He was a wealthy and well-respected man. When I moved in, he was erecting a gigantic duplex—one of the biggest in his community. People always stopped to look and admire the construction. Like the success post we see on social media, everyone who passed ascribed him as a very successful man. On one of the days I praised him for his accomplishments, he called me back and asked:

"How many years do you think it took me to save to build this house?"

I knew he was a former school teacher, and I understood that a couple of them were often either owed or underpaid. For that reason, I didn't think he became that affluent by teaching. He must have ventured into business. So I replied, "ten years, Sir."

He giggled and thereafter told me it took him thirty whole years. I froze in astonishment.

He added that I was not the only one who reacted that way. But then he is not able to fathom why it always comes as a surprise to people. It made sense to understand that nowadays, success has become so easy to acquire that thirty years is too long a time to grow into success. Hence the reason why ten years is enough for anyone *to blow* (become wealthy), as my fellow Nigerians will always say. He sat me down that day and began to narrate how he advanced from an underpaid school teacher who could barely afford a befitting home and food to a headmaster. Thirty whole years of his life was devoted to teaching. And essentially, it was during his teaching service year that he painstakingly saved, invested and planned his retirement. Though the times were tough on him, he made the decision to secure his retirement.

What his constructed duplex admirers and myself saw was success, achievements, accomplishment and more. There was no sign of the sacrifices and rough times he went through. Not until he told me, at least, I'd probably be wishing to own the same kind of house with zero willingness to walk in the worn-out shoes he walked in. It would also have sounded like motivational speaking if he posted the house pictures on social media. The comments you would likely see on the post would read like:

From nowhere, a school teacher builds a mansion. How did that happen?

Oh well it happened because he worked for it. However what is not visible is the posts on-board his journey to building this elegant mansion.

On this note, I wish to congratulate everyone who made it with no struggle—likewise, the "zero to hero" achievers. The goal was to succeed, and succeed we did. The world celebrates us.

Nonetheless, I wish to promote the idea of reading and learning from the road travelled.

Liken it to a football game where we watch and support our teams to win. And even in times of failure, also watching and encouraging them to train harder and rise again. The picture painted of success can be better if some "cached" background colours are highlighted.

Again, to the one on course to achieve, conquer or succeed: Note that one man's success is not the yardstick for another man's failure.

We are not late because our peers have arrived at the destination we long for.

We are not late because we got admitted into the university when our mates had already graduated.

We are not late because we are thirty and yet to start a professional career, while those in their early twenties are already growing a stable job.

In my opinion, we are only late when we fail to do what we have to do today to prepare for the tomorrow we desire.

I know not of one man in the world who has attained it all. So success inevitably has no end. It has the capacity to go round and still remain. The little we owe each other is a pat on the back, which in this case is advertising success more intentionally.

And for the rising reader, don't forget that gold is refined by fire. So, let the road you are travelling towards your dream build and prepare you for that future. As you celebrate your small wins, remember to accommodate the road travelled, not only the end destination.

13
You Will Surprise Yourself

Have you ever looked at someone´s result or achievement and asked yourself if they were created differently? Well, I have. One of such times was in High School. It was a holiday period, but our holiday class was ongoing. One lovely afternoon, my class instructor shared his A-level result with us in a bid to spice up the lesson. He had 2As, 1B, 2Cs (20/25 = 80%), with A grades in Pure Mathematics and Further Mathematics. At the time, I just could not imagine having an A-grade in Pure Mathematics or Further Mathematics. He must be a genius to have made such a result.

Out of curiosity, I approached after that class to ask how he achieved such spectacular results.

"If you work hard enough, you will surprise yourself", he told me.

Till today, this statement, as they say, lives "rent-free" in my head.

His counsel was very soothing as it emphasised studying more and never allowing oneself to become comfortable or falling into the delusion that "because it is difficult, it's undoable," more wisdom to my knowledge bank.

About one year later, my Advanced level GCE results were released and guess what? *E shock me!* (taken unaware) I was surprised to see my result, and everything he said made practical sense. I got a total of 23/25 points (4As, 1C), thereby achieving the best result from my high school and among the best in my region. The icing on the cake was the A-grades in Pure Mathematics and Further Mathematics.

Ahh! So I finally became that genius I saw in my instructor, interesting!

Another similar experience happened in Form Four during my secondary school days at Presbyterian Comprehensive High School (PCHS), Kumbo. Following the release of Form Five student's mock examination results, the best students in that class got 80% in Biology! Another genius act, no doubt. Biology was well known for its voluminous curriculum, so a B grade was good enough, but an A? how come? I asked myself. As usual, I went again to probe, and the genius league explained that it was possible through hard work. So, once more, I banked it and went to work.

One year later, it was my turn to take the Biology mock examination. During the exam, we were asked to answer four questions, each carrying 25 marks. Anyone could answer more than four questions, in which case the teacher selected the best four. However, this was not advisable because a student might not have sufficient time to give their best to more than four questions. Since I had some time to spare after answering four questions, I ended up with five questions in total.

When the results came out, I got 85%

I never experred it. (Didn't see it coming)

While taking a closer look at my script to understand how I arrived at such amazing result, I noticed my teacher had chosen the first four, whereas my fifth question had a higher score. I immediately went back to him to explain. He identified it as oversight and corrected it. I ended up having 90% following the update.

My learning from both experiences is the ability to believe that we can; if we are determined to pursue and conquer.

When I share how much confidence I have in my mentees, some are quick to ask why. Void of selection or preference, I coach my mentees. My principle is that mentorship is not for the smart alone but for those willing to get smart, stay smart and are intentional about their future.

No one is wholly a dullard. Mindsets and conditions can be changed, any time, any day.

Are you ready to surprise yourself?

THEME 4:
Life´s Imagination versus Reality

14
Take Me to School

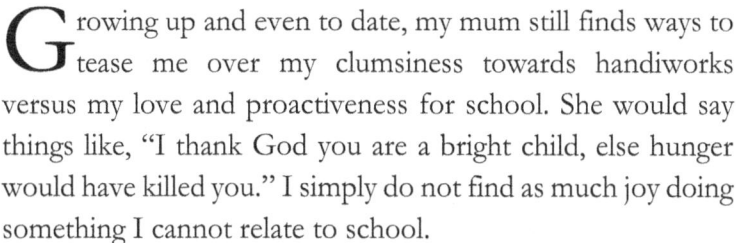

Growing up and even to date, my mum still finds ways to tease me over my clumsiness towards handiworks versus my love and proactiveness for school. She would say things like, "I thank God you are a bright child, else hunger would have killed you." I simply do not find as much joy doing something I cannot relate to school.

My childhood school memory is pretty funny but then says a lot about my flair for education.

At age four, my playmate had begun schooling. I would watch him step out each morning for school in his nicely ironed blue shorts and white shirt, with a cartoon-themed school bag on his back that was complemented with a cute lunchbox. He would wave me goodbye on his way out. I guess he also enjoyed my watch and admiration routine.

I enjoyed watching him and wished to be like him so badly. I wondered why I wasn't doing the same thing since we were age mates. So, one day, I walked up to my mother, who was

Life's Imagination versus Reality

busy preparing to head out to our business premises. I told her I wanted to start school. She gave me a long look and replied that I was too young for school.

"How can I be too young when my friend has already started school?" I asked.

She gave no reply and continued with her task. I was deeply hurt, and crying was the only way to express it, so I let it out. Initially, it was low key, but my heart was so heavy that the pitch skyrocketed within seconds. I cried so much that my mother had to yield to my proposal to have peace. She dressed me up, but before leaving the house, she said to me, "let it be on record that I gave it a chance, in case they don't admit you for the same reason I told you, your size."

I shouted, "yes, let's go. I will not blame you, mummy."

When we got to the school, it was like a dream come true. The fact that I made it to the school environment alone was already a win for me. I kept looking like I had come for sightseeing until we got to the headmistress's office. While my mother sat to explain why we had come, the headmistress gave me a long look as though she was measuring my height with her mind. She then informed my mother that I would need to take a readiness test to show if I qualify to start primary school. Her reason was that the ideal age for primary school was at least five years, and I was four. Contrary to their opinion, my prerequisite was my friend back home who started school at age four.

While still doing my innocent calculation, the headmistress's voice rang in my ears, "Can you touch your left ear with your right hand across your head?" She asked.

I immediately reached out to grab my ear, but no, I could not reach it. I tried many times, but my ear failed me. If only it could move an inch close to my hand, but it couldn't.

She then explained that I was just too young to be in primary school. My mother quickly turned to me with the "I told you so" look. Oh, I was hurt. How can my first school experience be a rejection? Why?

We left eventually. I didn't say a word to my mother to avoid any unfriendly reward for dragging her to school.

After many weeks of background checks, I discovered that my role model, my childhood friend, whom I always watched, started school from nursery and not primary school. I could not enrol like him because my parents could not afford it. Also, I needed to be at least five years old to start from the primary school they could afford.

Call it purpose or destiny; education holds a special place in my heart.

15
Not All Figured Out

The title you just read refers to none other than my humble self, Kelechukwu.

I agree that I work very hard to thrive in my career and that I inspire other people a lot to push through in like manner till everyone onboards the same thriving ship. It is also true that to achieve my visions and goals, I set up working standards and would not necessarily take no for an answer.

While it is good to show off these praiseworthy attributes, I deem it necessary also to spell out my limitations. In essence, I need you to understand that the same Kelechukwu you regard as a high achiever is the same Kelechukwu that is inevitably flawed by limitations.

Without my permission, life has taught me to learn and agree that I am not the one in control; God is. In detail, I have learned to stand still and give ground to waiting and believing. It is absolutely okay to have a lion spirit and thus exude courage and bravery. However, it also makes much meaning to come to terms with the fact that the heroic spirit's ability to produce certain results that we desire is limited.

In all sincerity, I can tell for a fact that there are major milestones in my life and career that I attained with incomplete to zero know-how. The only thing I did right was walk until the end of the road. I stopped to all intents and purpose where my efforts could not take me further. And it was too glaring to ignore that I made it to the expected end by grace and grace alone.

It is brightening for me to share the real-life experiences that occasioned my conclusion. I hope that it brings some level of reassurance to someone or anyone still feeling insufficient. No, you are not, and that is because no one has it all figured out, and it is okay.

My transition experience from Masters to PhD

I started my masters in the year 2013. As usual, the figured-out version of me had planned, based on standard procedure, to launch into my PhD program immediately after my masters. Since I started the master program (Erasmus Mundus Double Master) in 2013 and was to finish by 2015, my plan was, therefore, to secure a PhD position on or before the very end of the program. To that effect, I started to apply within the last few months of my master program.

Owing to my academic performance, I was pretty confident it would be easy-peasy to get a placement. Unfortunately, I was wrong, and it took four months for me to realise it.

I had begun making applications six months before my graduation. I made sure to apply every other day and was very optimistic that something would pop up. Based on confidence, I didn't bother about it. I instead paid more attention to my master thesis that I didn't realise when four months passed. Two months left, with no sign of a PhD offer? Interesting!

To compound the matter, I was to conclude my laboratory experiments, complete my thesis, and prepare for my master defence within the same two months. Again, my success in securing the PhD was to determine my residence in France. Implying that the only reason to remain in France was if I had a PhD placement. Outside of that, OYO (on your own) was my case. Relatively, one thing had to happen.

In a matter of months, which elapsed like Easter break, something I never thought would worry me became a nightmare.

"What was I to do?"

Thinking was readily available for use, but nothing came out of it. It made me worry even more. However, it was extremely difficult to avoid. It was a war within and outside my spirit. Only God can explain how I managed to bring my emotions under control.

Amidst all the issues I was anxious and angry about, the one that topped my list was the pile of rejection emails I received daily. It looked more like sending application letters was a prerequisite for rejection. Considering that I had no choice, I looked past the letters and continued to apply. I also informed my professors that I was in desperate need of a PhD position.

In a matter of days, one of the university professors indicated his interest in hiring me. But then he stated that he wasn't sure about securing the funding within the period. His earliest possible time was February 2016, which was way too late for me. I only had till July 2015. So the offer didn't sail.

At this point, I had exhausted all the efforts within reach, done everything I knew and was advised to do. From improving my curriculum vitae, cover letter, presentation of outstanding results and grades, writing to professors, I did them all. I tell you, nothing else was left to do.

It was at this point that I stood still. My toughness cum die-hard spirit was highly humbled. I feebly resorted to waiting and believing God.

A second breakthrough sufficed within the following weeks. My Master thesis supervisors agreed to hire me on the condition that I would apply for the university's annual PhD award.

So it happened that every year, the university awarded two PhD funding scholarships to top-performing MSc students within and outside the university. In other words, students within and outside of my university had equal opportunities to apply, which made it more competitive.

My amazing supervisors on this account honoured me by recommending me for the position. I immediately applied. I also continued to apply to other placements.

Two months ran into one and further to weeks till it was one week to my MSc defence. No description can equate to the level of anxiety I was feeling. Again only God can explain how I managed.

Five days to my MSc thesis defence, and my laboratory director sent for me. I didn't think about what and why he invited me. I just went. On getting to his office, he announced that I had advanced to the interview stage of the Marie-Curie EJD FunMat PhD program.

Marie what? I muttered

"The Marie-Curie EJD FunMat PhD programs", he replied.

It took me a while to recall that I had applied to the Marie-Curie EJD FunMat PhD position (EJD-FunMat: European Joined Doctoral in Functional Materials). How could I have remembered when I had made hundreds of applications. Let alone seeing that it was a well-known and highly competitive PhD position. I also must have applied for the sake of it and not necessarily because I felt I could get through.

Oh my, it was surreal. I never expected it.

He further explained that I was among the final eight selected from over a hundred applicants.

Wow! How did I get here?

Another surprising thing was finding out that he was one of the two supervisors for the Marie-Curie EJD FunMat project I had applied to on "sustainable derivatisation of cellulose in ionic liquids"

Two major surprises in one day. Whether or not I was going to get the position didn't matter. Making it to the top eight was in no way a *"drink water, drop cup"* matter. I considered myself a hero and was highly encouraged to be steadfast.

I left his office feeling like a crown prince. My dear friend would add "Kutuku land" in this case. Yes, I felt like the crown prince of Kutuku land (imaginary wonderland) with my shoulder hanging high up like the eagle's wing.

Finally, grace found me.

As King Solomon said in the book of proverbs 3:5-6, "Trust in the Lord with all your heart, lean not on your understanding, in all your ways acknowledge Him, and He shall direct your steps."

Oh my God!

To think that God continued where I stopped to bring me to this expected end made me very emotional.

It's possible that I walk-danced back home, but I didn't care. The child in me was out to give thanks.

You may be wondering why my excitement was overboard.

The reason is that firstly I never thought I could be selected. Second, I was told my chances were slimmer during the application, considering that I was a former beneficiary of a similar European Union funding for my masters. So my application was purely for the sake of it.

Fast forward to the next steps, I was to have a final interview with the host professor from the coordinating University, Karlsruhe Institute of technology, KIT-Germany.

Tick tock, time passed till two days to my Master thesis defence. I opened my mailbox that morning to an email from the KIT professor requesting to schedule the final interview for the PhD funding. The date he suggested unfortunately clashed with the day of my thesis defence. Regardless, I accepted without even mentioning it to him. Wasn't sure how

I was going to manage both events, but there was no room to take any chances.

The interview was scheduled for 9:30 am, while my master thesis defence was for 12:30 pm. On the set day, I prepared and went in for my interview. While it was ongoing, I humbly clarified to the professor that I was defending that same day at 12:30 pm.

He was astonished and asked why I didn't say earlier, adding that he would have rescheduled. I replied that I didn't want to risk the chance. He was highly impressed with my response and attitude.

Eventually, I completed the interview, and he told me to expect the outcome in a few days since he still had to interview other candidates.

I immediately hurried down to my master thesis defence venue, revising my presentation underway. I defended at about 12:30 pm, and it was great. I walked out of the defence room feeling fulfilled.

Unknown to me, there was more. The head of the Chemistry Institute, who coincidentally was part of my defence jury, called to inform me that I emerged first on the top list of candidates for the University of Bordeaux PhD funding. The same one they recommended for me.

I went into shock. Like I was literally shaking. I quickly said a prayer of thanksgiving as in Psalms 97:12, "Rejoice in the Lord, you righteous, and give thanks at the remembrance of His holy name."

Lord, I thank you.

The professor continued by saying that all that was required of me was a "yes."

How did I get here? What a dream come true.

Dear reader,

Peradventure, you are currently going through some uncommon experience, I encourage you to reflect on my case and further believe that your limitation is not the end of the story. Secondly, no matter what background you came from or how unimaginable your dreams are, it is valid and possible with you and God.

Now, back to my story.

I had to respond to the offer immediately, but then I decided to give it a thought first. Considering that the Marie-Curie PhD offer was also in view. So I asked for a few days to think and get back.

"Okay, Kenny, but you have to decide within two days as we have to finalise this selection," the Chemistry institute head replied.

As if they knew, I got home that evening to an email from the Marie-Curie PhD funding stating my position as the topmost candidate on their list. Unlike the other offer, they needed a few days to reveal their final decision to me.

Like play, it struck me that I had transited from "no certain PhD offer" to "which PhD offer."

The Psalms: When the Lord turned again the captivity of Zion, we were like them that dream played out in my head like a movie.

Indeed, God is faithful!

Once upon a time, I was unsure what the next steps to take were. The only thing I was sure to do was return to my home country whether or not I wanted it.

And now? "Chukwuewerugo onodu" (God has taken over)

Since I now had two options to consider, I had to decide which one was best for me carefully. So I sought counsel. My elder brother happened to be my best option. As a result, I reached out to him. He was more than happy to help. On explaining the situation, he suggested that I outline the factors that I considered paramount to acquiring a satisfying PhD. Afterwards, I attach a score to each of the factors for each PhD offer. And in the end, sum up the scores and go for the offer with the highest score. He was such a wise man, and his constructive game theory was helpful.

I analysed the offers as directed and thoroughly contemplated which offer stood out. I recall a specific factor on my list called "adaptation." I wanted to be in a research group that would be easier to adapt. The offer to stay back in Bordeaux ranked high since I would stay with the same fantastic supervisors from my master's thesis. In contrast, the Marie-Curie offer meant that I would have to move to Germany and commence with a new research group.

Another factor was accommodation. The Bordeaux offer ranked higher since I could keep my current accommodation than searching for a new place in Karlsruhe. Moreover, the offer from Bordeaux would allow me to extend my French visa, thus saving me from the stress of applying for a visa from Nigeria, which the Marie-Curie option would have required. I also considered the stipend payable by each funding and the Marie-Curie was a clear winner in this category.

When I considered all these critical factors, the Bordeaux offer was indeed my clear comfort zone. So the opportunity cost and quid pro quo of accepting the Bordeaux offer was sacrificing the Marie-Curie funding.

It is worth mentioning that the University of Bordeaux funding went to the candidate, not the laboratory. Therefore, declining the offer would deny my master thesis supervisors the opportunity to continue with the research topic I was working on in my master thesis. It was indeed one of the most challenging decisions I had ever made.

I did a lot of thinking. Most times, I stayed up thinking and analysing, considering so many things simultaneously. It was just not easy to decide.

Eventually, I resorted to prayer. Being confident that God's guidance was the best. I prayed, asking for guidance and direction. I asked that He directs me to the place where His grace would carry me. I found my peace as expected when the idea of leaving my comfort zone came to mind, and that was it. I decided to leave Bordeaux.

In furtherance of my decision, I forwarded my rejection letter to my university and supervisors.

On the other hand, I emailed the host professor for the Marie-Curie offer, stating that I was willing to accept their offer. They didn't ask for the response, they were to tell me, but I went ahead to send my unrequested response.

Call it a leap of faith, and you'd be right.

I switched off my laptop afterwards and tried to sleep. My mind needed to rest, but then I struggled back and forth with scenarios playing in my mind. It felt terrible knowing how hard my professors pushed me to apply for the Bordeaux position. I could not imagine how disappointed they would feel after reading my rejection letter. After a roller coaster of wild thoughts, I opened up my computer in wait for their reply.

One by one, they popped in up. I could not summon the courage to read any till the next day.

I opened the first one, and behold, it was the opposite of what I expected. I went on with the rest, and it read the same. They all clearly expressed their shock about my decision. However, the remaining 90% of the emails were filled with congratulatory messages and best wishes. Meanwhile, they had no idea I was still waiting for final offer reply for the Marie-Curie funded PhD. My faith arose much more that the tiny nerves I was having vanished.

Days after, I got the feedback, and it was a resounding yes and this was how my Marie-Curie ITN double PhD program in Functional Materials journey started.

For what it's worth, I did all I could, but it was clearly not enough. It does not translate to being a failure but instead makes it pellucid that I am human and can only do all things through God, who strengthens me.

No one has it all figured out, provided you have given it all, all you can do is to wait, and keep being positive.

No one has it all figured out, except you are the one watching your back when you are facing front.

16

Experiences: What Counts is What You Do with Them

Who can predict life or what it brings forth? We as humans have done and still doing a lot to control certain factors, yet life has not for once ceased to amaze us. Covid-19 pandemic is a good enough example.

Despite what life we have or what it brings our way, we find ways to adapt and carry on. Whether or not we are defeated, life goes on eventually. So many have gone, many are still here, life has continued. In between what we have or leave behind are experiences and memories.

Experience may not define who we are or become; nonetheless, it tells each person's unique story. Life experience is the best teacher, says David Letterman. Best teacher for the one who went through it and another who makes meaning out of it. Many years later, the world still shares his unique journey through life; his experiences.

Life's Imagination versus Reality

In 2018, when I was a 2nd year PhD candidate, I was blessed to be selected among the 30 Marie-Curie finalists to participate in the Falling Wall Lab competition in Brussels, Belgium.

The Falling Wall lab is a science fair competition to showcase the innovative research works by scientists worldwide that are capable of breaking down various walls. The finals of the event took place in Berlin, Germany, between the winners of the different categories. Marie-Curie Fellows was one of the categories that competed at the final. The selection of the Marie-Curie representative took place through an intensive competition between 30 candidates, including me. Before the D-day, and within three days, we were trained on various public speaking skills. In addition, I was opportune to practice communicating skills to a non-science audience and time management. We were allowed to use only one slide to communicate our PhD research below a record time of three minutes (180 seconds) for the presentation. 2.30 minutes was for the presentation and 30 seconds for questions and answers. I don't remember practising hard for any presentation as I did for this competition. I had to know precisely the right words owing to the time factor. I practised to the point where I could recite my presentation in my dream.

The final day came, and I mounted the stage and presented my research work with all the passion in me. There was thunderous applause, I felt no matter what happened, and even if I didn't get the best award, I would clinch one of the four prizes available. The final moment of truth came after everyone had presented, and the winners were called one after another. I waited with my heart beating as if I had just completed a 100 meters sprint. Then, the fourth and final prize winners were called, and I wasn't among them. I was sad to have lost out and spent the next hours failing to understand why I didn't win any of the awards. I thought I nailed it, but obviously, the other 25 contestants that were not selected thought the same.

That evening as I lay on my bed, the competition kept playing in my mind. Finally, I concluded that I might not have won any awards but undoubtedly gained some experience by being part of the competition. In addition, I had the opportunity to broaden my network and equally learned how to communicate technical research to a non-science audience.

Two days after this competition, I was to deliver an oral presentation at a scientific conference in Karlsruhe, Germany. The audience was different from the one at the Falling Wall lab, and instead of three minutes, we were given twenty minutes for the presentation. Somehow the previous experience came in the way as I struggled to practice longer than three minutes. I guess my brain already programmed itself to shorten presentation to the barest minimum following the countless practice I did for the three minutes presentation. Practising for longer talks became quite challenging.

I managed to prepare for my talk eventually. So came the D-day, and once it was my turn, I took the stage and delivered a fantastic presentation. The applause was thunderous, and I got amazing feedbacks. When I met my German supervisor after the talk, he shook my hands and said I did a fantastic job. Looking at the energy and the passion I demonstrated during the presentation, no one would believe if I told how difficult it was for me to prepare & deliver my talk just two days after losing the competition in Brussels.

This experience, in conclusion, taught me how better to manage my losses. No matter how hard they hit, pressing forward should remain a constant.

Our experiences should not become an obstacle we try to surmount but instead a bridge to cross over to new feats. With such mindset, we are sure to become unstoppable.

So my question to you reader is, "what tools are you making out of your experiences?" Are those tools enabling you to do it differently next time?

17

Delay Can Be a Redirection

I defended my PhD on 4th February 2019, after days, weeks and months of intense work accompanied by travelling all over Europe and the USA for conferences. Though I defended in February, my Marie-Curie ITN funding contract ended the month before. I was only fortunate to receive an additional three-month contract until the end of April from my supervisor at KIT Germany, hence, I had to find another position/job once that expired.

Long before this time, I had begun searching and applying to several postdoc positions. Providentially for me, one of the professors in my research cluster had an exciting postdoc position in Liege, Belgium and proposed it to me. We had an interesting interview, and a few days later, I got the official acceptance for the position to start on 1st May 2019. Pumped for the new beginning, I ferociously began my Belgium visa processing.

The following week, I received an email from Procter & Gamble stating I had been selected to join their highly competitive four-day PhD Seminar scheduled for the 24th-27th of March. Attending their PhD seminar was more like a step forward in their job application process. It was one of the positions I applied in December 2018 just barely 6 weeks before my PhD defense. I also did their interview in January 2019. Though I was expectant, I wasn't keen on it since I had already got an offer for postdoc in Belgium.

Notwithstanding, I decided to attend. At best, it will allow me to meet and connect with new people and learn more about the company.

Time flew quickly while I intensely pursued my Belgium visa that 24th March came faster than expected. Nevertheless, I made sure to attend the entire four days of the seminar despite the other issues I was handling. To my utmost surprise, the event turned out better than I envisioned. Quite insightful, I was pleased to have attended.

Still bubbling in the recent turn of events, I was already picturing a perfect and easy future. Yet, serious crises were awaiting my arrival at the forefront, unknown to me. Let me explain.

After the P&G PhD seminar, I continued with my Belgium visa application. One of the many strenuous requirements for this visa was the medical certification process. It involved running many medical tests. These tests took me from one end of Karlsruhe to the other. Getting a doctor's appointment alone took a whole month. Lucky me, the doctor only needed to sign a medical certificate if all my results were OK. What was critical was to have all the required medical tests completed before the doctor's appointment scheduled towards the end of March. Finally, I finished all the medical tests and attended the doctor's appointment. He went through all the medical reports, was satisfied, and signed two copies of the medical certificates.

To resume my postdoc offer on 1st May, I needed to have my visa ready latest 30th April 2019. Considering that it took the Belgian embassy two to four weeks for visa processing, I needed to submit my application on or before 30th March.

It was already the third week of March; after what seemed like an endless struggle, I wrapped up and submitted my application by post to the Belgian embassy in Berlin. And the waiting began.

On the other hand, the end of the 3-month KIT contract from my supervisor was just a month away. Another complication was that my residence permit for Germany was due to expire within the same period, 30th April precisely. So it was either I secured the Belgium Visa or renewed my German Visa. How convenient, phew!

What was the point of renewing my German visa, knowing I would be relocating to Belgium for my postdoc? No reason, aside from my intention to travel to Nigeria, I renewed it anyway, for six months to have a valid permit for the trip. And I continued waiting for my Belgian visa.

The next struggle was the waiting process. Everything I submitted was through the post, and there was no response on reception. The one and only option were to wait. No day passed without me checking my email at least ten times, hoping to receive a notification that my visa was ready. As the day passed, so did my tension and confusion increase. The month of March ended so fast I wondered if my frustration was causing the days to "fly". Oh, how much I had wished the days went by slower!

One fateful afternoon in mid-April, I got a call from Procter & Gamble.

"We have a position that we think fits your profile based on your interest submitted during the PhD seminar. Will you be willing to be interviewed?"

"Yes," I replied immediately.

Two days later, I got an invitation link to attend an online interview. During this first interview, the hiring manager briefed me on Research and Development, Packaging position. I was interested in the job and the company's drive towards more sustainable packaging. Sustainability was a big motivation of my PhD research that focused on developing advanced materials from renewable resources (cellulose). It was pretty interesting for me as it was relatable to the bio-based cellulose transparent film (potential packaging material) developed during my research.

After the first interview, I got an email later that I had progressed to the last phase and was invited for another interview at the P&G technical centre close to Frankfurt, Germany. During this interview, I started by presenting my PhD thesis, followed by a series of situational-based and peak performance interviews. After the discussion, I asked the hiring manager when to expect the final decision. His response shocked me to my bones. He immediately replied that he was happy to hire me if I wanted to join his team.

I might not have processed what he had said and only truly realised that I had just gotten my first full-time job outside academia when I got to the train station. The response I got was the best regarding a permanent job offer. However, some processes were still to be followed to confirm the job offer. Amidst my euphoria, I recalled what a P&G employee told me at that point, "till you have your offer in your hand and sign the contract, nothing is cast on stone."

I immediately coordinated myself, went home and continued my postdoc preparation while expecting a call or email from the Belgian embassy regarding my visa. Asides from the visa issue, I was already in possession of the signed postdoc work contract; hence the only offer already cast on stone. Being hopeful that the Belgian visa would soon arrive, I went ahead to pay for my accommodation in Liege, Belgium. In addition, I gave up my accommodation in Karlsruhe, Germany, getting ready to travel to Belgium on 30th April 2019 latest. However, as the date drew nearer, I was increasingly bothered about the silence from the Belgian embassy.

Tick tock, tick tock, and it was 29th April already. You can only imagine my state of confusion at this point.

Did I make any mistakes on my visa application?

Did I miss any documents?

Did I submit it wrongly?

A ton of questions ran through my mind. To worsen my situation, I couldn't find a way to contact the embassy to check on the status of my visa application. I had written them a series of emails but no response. Then it dawned on me that I was gradually becoming homeless in Germany and directionless.

The one decision I made that turned out to be my lifesaver was to renew my German Visa, which I did to enable my travel to Nigeria and not necessarily to stay in Germany. Remember, I already gave out my accommodation in Germany as of 30th April and my accommodation in Liege Belgium was to begin from 1st May.

"I should be in Liege Belgium by now", I fumed as I paced endlessly in my Karlsruhe apartment that I was to give up the next day.

The Belgian visa delay frustrated me beyond measure. What was I going to do? I asked myself with no answer in mind. I trusted the Belgian Consulate so much that I didn't consider making alternative plans. I could have kept my Karlsruhe apartment at the least.

Homeless in Germany, Ahh, why me!

How long was I to wait to finally get the decision on my visa from the Belgian embassy? I already paid rent in Liege; where do I go from here? I wondered in frustration.

What sort of distressing delay is this? I asked myself over and over.

Within this same time, I was to attend the finals of the Germany Famelab Science competition scheduled for 6th May 2019 in Bielefeld which I qualified as one of the two winners from the regional finals. Furthermore, I also had to give an oral presentation at one of the biggest international conferences that were to take place in LaRochelle, France, from 13th May 2019. Therefore, I had to factor both engagements into any plans I was to make.

I thought hard and long with my already packed luggage. It was a matter of some hours before the new tenant was to move in, yet I had no idea what I would do afterwards.

At this moment, I had a serious rethink about the entire decision to move to Belgium. I felt sad that I had to still go through such a rigorous and painful visa application process even after spending five years in Europe. It is important to note that staying outside of Germany for longer than six months would lead to losing the entire time gained in the past. Moving to Belgium would cause me to lose the three years I already stayed in Germany by that time. Considering that I would be eligible for Germany permanent resident (PR) status if I stayed back in Germany for further two years, making a total of five years, I decided not to take the postdoc offer. Initially, I never considered staying back in Germany. However, visa delay coupled with the trauma and associated cost I incurred during this period led to my change of heart.

My colleagues were shocked when I informed them that I was not taking the postdoc offer.

"How will you manage in Germany? they asked. "I will get a job," I replied.

"How can that be? You speak little or no German. You, of all people, have witnessed how long it took our PhD counterparts, even Germans themselves, to obtain permanent job offers; how do you intend to beat that." I understood their concerns, and sincerely I was scared. Regardless, my mind was made, not after coming close to becoming an illegal migrant in Germany and going through the trauma of applying and waiting for the Belgium visa.

It was tough for me to inform the Belgium professor about my decision to decline the offer, but I did eventually. They were already waiting for my resumption from 1st May 2019 with my laboratory space and work desk prepared. I explained as clearly as I could, but I understood what a big blow it was to him, considering the amount of effort to get the funding for such projects.

I was so lost in thought but immediately stood up when I heard a knock on the door. The new tenant finally arrived. I honestly can't tell how I managed to speak to him. I humbly and helplessly explained my predicament and pleaded with him to share the apartment on split rent until the end of May.

Sadly, but of course, as expected, he declined the proposal. He was just moving in. Such inconvenience cannot be taken easily by someone on first meeting. But he was kind enough to let me stay till 6th May just in time for my competition at the Germany Famelab finals. Fast-forward to the morning of the competition, I packed my most important belongings into a small travelling bag and left the rest in his care and travelled to Bielefeld, Germany.

The finals went quite well, and I presented to a crowd of over one thousand people. The British Council organisers uploaded all the presentations from the competition on their YouTube channel. Funny as it might sound, just looking at my presentation wouldn't give you a glimpse of all the uncertainties I was going through.

After the competition, I had nowhere to stay before my next engagement being the international scientific conference in La Rochelle, France, from the 13th to the 17th of May.

Eventually, I decided to go on a week-long vacation to Vienna, Austria, to at least pass time there, clear my head on the next rational move to make. I instantly boarded a train from Bielefeld to Karlsruhe and took a 13 hours bus trip to Vienna. I searched online for a youth hostel in Vienna and made payments for seven nights.

On the 2nd day of my vacation, I attended a Ballet performance at the famous Opera House in Vienna. It was spectacular, and after the first performance, I got a beep on my phone and hurriedly checked as soon as I had a chance. Guess what it was? My P&G offer with a proposed resumption date for 1st July 2019. This news filled me with all sorts of emotions, and my joy knew no bounds! I had just lived through the past weeks with all its uncertainties. I could now see the light at the end of the tunnel with this offer.

17.1 Not over, till it is over

After receiving my P&G contract in Vienna, I decided to visit the city of my childhood dream, Budapest-Hungary. It was just about three hours from Vienna. I enjoyed myself so much in Budapest that I was beginning to forget all the stressful previous weeks. My next stopover was La Rochelle, France, as my self-imposed vacation finally ended. My wonderful PhD supervisor in France registered me for the conference and paid for a trip by train from Karlsruhe to Paris. I took the bus from Vienna and arrived in Karlsruhe around 3:00 am and had to wait at the train station for my train to La Rochelle, which had a change-over in Paris. The train to Paris was to leave Karlsruhe at about 7:30 am.

Then another disaster struck, being so tired from the 13 hours bus trip from Vienna to Karlsruhe. I had just gotten myself a hot chocolate at the train station in Karlsruhe and was about to relax to drink when it occurred to me that I was not with my travelling bag. This bag contained most of my valuable possession. I had not brought it down from the bus. Oh my, Kelechukwu!

I ran immediately after the bus as fast as my feet could carry me, but that was not enough to meet the bus; it left already and headed for Paris. I checked the bus route and found out that the expected arrival time in Paris was 11.30 am. My train to Paris was scheduled to arrive at about 10.45 am, while my booked connecting train to La Rochelle was to leave the Paris train station by 11.30 am.

I was not myself on the train from Karlsruhe to Paris.

"What if someone who has an earlier stop before Paris mistakenly takes my bag?" I asked myself.

Eventually, I got to Paris and got to the main bus terminal just in time to wait for the bus's arrival. I waited for about 20 minutes before the bus arrived, and thanks to God, my bag was still there. So I picked it up and walked out of the bus station as nothing had happened. Only God would know how worried and disturbed I was.

When I got back to the Paris central train station, I had to pay for another ticket to La Rochelle since my earlier train had left. But, for me, this extra fair was nothing compared to the bag I recovered.

After the conference at La Rochelle, the next step was to find accommodation close to my place of work in Frankfurt. I called one of our family friends in Frankfurt and explained my situation to him. He was super helpful and said I could stay at his place for the week till I got my place. Later that night, I arrived at his home and had a very restful sleep, one after such a long while.

I emailed and called some of the accommodation contacts that P&G shared with me, but none were positive. I remember my family friend mentioning how difficult it would be to get accommodation in Frankfurt. The second day, I made some more calls, and one of them accepted that I could come and check an apartment. Upon visiting, I liked the apartment, and I was able to sign the contract on the spot. I booked my flight to Nigeria that same evening, and by 29th May 2019, I was in Nigeria with my family. Finally, I could rest and enjoy three weeks of vacation.

As I look back at this experience, I return Glory to God. How else do I explain how I went through such a terrifying period. As someone who believes wholly in God, I always made sure to pray and remind myself of God's faithfulness throughout the ordeal. Unknown to me, what I perceived as a delay was a redirection.

The lesson I can share with the reader is to continuously assess what is being communicated to them by the delay they are experiencing.

Don't be too quick to conclude or give up following a challenging situation, especially when you cannot do much to change it. Something best might just be waiting for you at the next push; your duty, therefore, is to keep going.

That delay might just be a redirection for good, you just read my story.

THEME 5:
Persistence & Resilience

18
Rebel intent; life lessons learnt

"Mummy, I am neither staying back nor continuing my studies here. I have made up my mind to move to Nigeria." I didn't care what repercussion my actions would bring me, I could not hold back my anger and feeling of disappointment.

Prior to the time, my parents and I had agreed that I would be moving to Nigeria after my secondary school only to receive contrary news just few days to school resumption. My mum informed me after she noticed I wasn't planning for school resumption. This implied she and my dad had already decided long ago that I would continue with high school in Cameroon.

Poor me, I had already tabled my plan for schooling in Nigeria. Why would my parents do this to me? I kept wondering. In the end, the only way I was going to continue high school in Cameroon was if I was allowed to choose the school I wanted.

Let me give a bit of background that led to this encounter. After completing my primary education, I went to

Presbyterian Comprehensive High School, Kumbo (PCHS) Cameroon, where I spent five years until my Ordinary Level GCE. The arrangement with my parents was to return to Nigeria afterwards to take the JAMB (Joint Admission Matriculation Body) exam, an entrance examination to universities in Nigeria. However, when the time finally came, my parents changed plans. I did see their reasons but couldn't understand why I was the one made to stay back, unlike my siblings, who moved much earlier.

At this time, my youngest brother and I were the only ones left in Cameroon with our parents. My other siblings were already back in Nigeria. My parents felt I would burden my eldest sister, who accommodated my siblings in Nigeria. She, at the time, had just gotten married, and they thought it would be too much on her.

Though it was a good reason, I just could not come to terms with it, not after everything I had done, like the signing out rite. As was the tradition, when anyone was passing out of school or relocating, the other students would sign on their uniforms, more like a local way of doing send forth. I had already gone through the send forth tradition and could not imagine going back to the same school. Not to mention the recent disappointment I had just gone through with my first love experience as shared earlier in this book. My only option was to choose a different school. Because I was head bent on going to Nigeria, I decided to select a school that my mum would disapprove and that was Government Bilingual High School, Kumbo (GBHS).

As expected, my mother overruled the GBHS idea.

"You are not going to that school," she resounded.

Then let me *"jejely"* (quietly) move to Nigeria, I replied.

The rebel in me was out, and I wasn't going to change my mind. After some consideration, she agreed that I go and check the admission process.

Unknown to me, she only agreed because she knew getting admitted into the school was quite difficult. The plan was to allow me to try and return to say it didn't work out. Besides, my cousin tried to gain admission into the school for weeks with no luck. Much worse, the admission cycle in the school was already closed. So why waste time convincing me? I'll see things for myself and, in the end, return to my previous school, PCHS Kumbo.

The next day, I left for GBHS Kumbo. On arrival, I went straight to the admission office notice board. Behold, it was boldly written: ADMISSIONS ARE OVER, PLEASE DO NOT INSIST! The notice dated back to September 2005, and there I was, a week late. I was helpless. To avoid embarrassment, I left the admission office and started heading home. A few meters away from the gate, I came across someone headed for the school. My first thought was that he must be a teacher at the school or maybe a non-academic staff, either way, I wished to speak to him.

In the heat of the moment, I summoned the courage to approach him.

"Good morning Sir, sorry to bother you. I had come for admission into this school but read the notice that the admission cycle was closed for high school (Lower Sixth Science, LSS)." While still speaking, I extended my O-Level

GCE result to him. I could see a smile form on his face as he skimmed through my result, and then he asked if I had spoken to anyone at the school.

I said no.

With my results in his hand, he asked that I follow him back to the school. As we stepped through the school gate, a rather tall man with a mean demeanour shouted at the top of his voice,

"We are not accepting any new students, the classes are already very full." (I learnt later that this was the Vice Principal Academics). The teacher with me ignored (or rather acted like he didn't hear him) and still approached him.

Good morning Sir, he greeted and handed over my result to him. The look on his face changed. A smile formed around his lips, although he tried to conceal it.

"Why are you coming for admission this late?" He asked.

"I was sick, Sir," I lied.

Why not return to your former school? They'll be happy to have you, he continued.

For a moment, I was lost on what to say.

"My parents are unable to afford the boarding fee at my former school," I responded.

In between, my heart was beating like that of an athlete who had just finished a marathon.

"Well, let me see what I can do, but I cannot guarantee you anything.

Wait outside the gate," he said with a stern look.

The teacher who brought me left for his class while l stepped out of the school premises and waited outside the gate.

It was a long wait as I waited from about 10 am to 2 pm. While waiting, my cousin seeking admission into this same school met me. She was surprised to see me there and asked if I was there for admission reasons or to meet with someone.

Admission, I responded. She laughed hysterically; you know that type of laughter that says, "are you kidding me?"

"Admissions stopped over a week ago. I've been frequenting the school for the same reason for weeks now with no results, and you honestly think you will get it by standing outside the gate for hours."

"Well, I was asked to wait here, and that's what I'll do," I replied.

She wished me luck and went her way.

2.30 pm, the school was over. I watched the student and staffs troop out in batches until the last student with no sign of the Vice-principal. I continued waiting until about 4 pm. Finally, the Vice Principal walked out the gate and was quite surprised to see me still waiting.

To me, it felt like he had put me through a test to see how determined I was towards getting admission. I was just about to explain how I didn't mind waiting when he handed me my admission letter and asked that I make the fee payment the next day.

Unbelievable! I screamed, thank you, Sir.

Who would believe I got my admission letter on my first visit to the school? My mother was in for a shock.

I joyfully marched straight to our business premises afterwards. My uncle and mother received me as if I had just returned from a hunt. My mother explained that they were already getting worried since I took longer to return. I smiled as I approached her and handed my admission letter.

"The deal is sealed, mum. I got admitted into the school."

She was indeed shocked. For starters, she didn't expect me, a 17-year-old, to manage this independently. She had called my uncle to request his help to accompany me to the school. Alas, here I was with an admission letter in my hand. An admission that had taken my cousin several weeks with no positive outcome—goodness gracious!

I do not consider it luck, nor 100% perseverance; let us say: a little bit of push, determination, focus, patience and faith got me what I wanted. Thank God my parents were kinder, else my rebel would have ended badly. Nonetheless, I know better now and realised that a chance not taken is 100% chances lost.

19
Thanks, but I Will Take My Chances

"Is he expecting you?" asked the kind-hearted security officer at a pharmaceutical company in Lagos when I told him the QA (Quality Assurance) manager would be pleased to meet me. Although stunned by the tenacity of a 'small' man making such an outrageous request, the security man was kind enough to ring the QA manager, who agreed that he should allow me in. Let's take a step back to understand what led to this encounter.

It was June 2010. As a 4th year undergraduate, it was mandatory to undergo a 6-months internship. So, I made it to Lagos, carrying a letter of recommendation for Soulmate Industries from my Head of Department. In addition, one of my lecturers had given me the name of his friend who was working at Friesland Company (manufacturers of Peak Milk in Nigeria) at the time. "To kill both birds with the same stone," I decided to visit Friesland Company first before proceeding to Soulmate Industries since both companies were in Ikeja, Lagos. On getting to Friesland Company that fateful morning, the security man informed me that the person I was looking for was on vacation and would not be back until a couple of weeks. So, I left Friesland company and was headed to Soulmate Industries when I saw the signpost of a pharmaceutical company that one of my lecturers worked with in the past. When I approached the gate and told the security man that the QA manager would be pleased to meet me, he was indeed startled.

Eventually, the QA manager asked that I be granted access, and I was led to his office. "Young man, what can I do for you," he questioned. I handed over my CV to him and responded that I was looking for an internship placement. Before flipping through my CV, he kept muttering that there were no internship positions. They had just offered someone the last slot the previous week, he said. I stayed put while watching him flip through my CV and then my student transcript. He looked pleased after going through my documents. "Come with me," he said and led me to the Human Resource manager's office. With my results in his hand, he moved from one office to the next, seeking to create a position for me. After what seemed like an endless journey, he returned 20 minutes later and announced that they would consider me for an internship position by the beginning of the following month (July 2010). I thanked him and dashed out the door, headed to my initial destination, Soulmate Industries, where I submitted my application too. By the following week, I got an invitation to interview at Soulmate Industries. First, there was an assessment test in which I scored over 90%. I was interviewed and told that they would contact me soonest. As I made my way to the door, a staff member called me back and said I should proceed to medicals. And by Wednesday of that same week, I got a call to start my internship the following week. That's not all. Just a few days into my internship at Soulmates Industries, I got a call from the previous pharmaceutical company I had visited to start my internship the following week.

It all seemed like a dream because I had received a lot of discouragement from my course mates before coming to Lagos for the hunt. A couple of them already in Lagos had told me that every IT slot in Lagos was filled-up, and there is no internship placement even if I came with a recommendation. Therefore, I shouldn't bother coming at all. Yes, I heard the warning, but I was unwilling to sit back and not try because others said so. I will take my chance! That was the only thing in my head. And thankfully, I got two internship positions within two weeks of arriving in Lagos. Once again, let me reiterate, no chance taken is 100% chances lost.

20
Not For Less

Our background quickly places us at the mercy of settling for less. When I did my first internship in 2008, I was paid 3000 naira ($20 equivalence as of then) per month for three months. Eventually, I got paid 5000 naira in total, but I was happy because I gained a valuable skill for free (how to produce wall paints). When I was interviewed two years later (2010) for a six-month internship, they asked how much I was paid in my last internship. I felt ashamed to share; perhaps they might pay me the same. However, I learned that this new company had a fixed intern stipend of 12000 naira ($80) per month. I remember how excited and happy I was when I received my first-month salary. This excitement will soon start eroding because my intern colleagues and I were already agitating for an increased stipend in the second month. Two years later (2012), as a Youth Corper, participating in the Nigeria's compulsory one year service for all her graduates, I was paid a stipend of 19,800 naira ($125) per month. In addition, I was doing some extra side jobs, which augmented my monthly salary to 35,000 naira ($225) per month. With such an income, I couldn't be any happier; at least, I thought. In 2013 I got my first real job as Graduate Assistant in my Alma mater with a monthly salary of over 100,000 naira (> $625 then). I remember calling my older brother to share my excitement. While he joined me in the celebration of achieving such a feat before my 25th birthday, he made sure to leave me with one statement to ponder upon, "don't lose sight of the big picture because of today's offer." I took his advice to heart and ensured not to become comfortable with where I was. This paid out eventually; as a few months later, I won an 18000 euros scholarship to join the Erasmus Mundus Masters program. Two years after (2015), I won a three-year European Union Marie-Curie ITN PhD funding worth over 150,000,000 naira ($360,000) that covered my research expenses and supported me with a monthly stipend for the entire three years.

In retrospect, if I did not have an older brother who had walked such a path before, that kept reminding me not to be comfortable when I felt I had "arrived," I could have quickly settled for less. Besides, how can you picture something that you cannot envision? As a teenager, I didn't imagine one person could earn so much simply by being a high academic performer till my older brother got admitted to FUTO. Here, he won the Shell-Agip undergraduate scholarship as a FUTO student that paid him about 75.000 naira in 2000 ($880) for his entire five years of studies. Upon graduation, he won the Erasmus Mundus scholarship after working for Procter & Gamble for two years. He was indeed the light that shone at the end of the tunnel, allowing me to find my path through the limitations that my background could have otherwise hindered.

Our background, in my opinion, can do us double tragedy, first as a limitation to what we can achieve today and secondly as an obstacle to what we can achieve tomorrow. Our background can lead us to question if we are worth more, we can't even imagine earning six figures in dollars or more.

My take-home advice here is that we should never feel our background can limit us on how far we can go. First, take a moment & picture what you can become and earn, do so by shadowing those in your field or the field you intend to grow into, those who have broken the limit of their background. Learn about their lives, what they did differently, what training and exposure did they get? Be reminded that you can also do the same if someone else has done it before. The basis of overcoming our background limitation is HOPE that the future we picture can exist. Be practical on how you want to bring this future picture into reality. The road doesn't promise to be all rosy, but that's the beauty of life so that when you finally get this future picture into a reality, you will appreciate the road travelled. Eventually, remember that as long as you can picture it, you can live it, as long as you are willing to go through the process.

Yes, you can be more than the background you are coming from.

THEME 6:
The Light in Failure

21
What Does Failure Mean to You?

"Kelechukwu Onwukamike: 4 out of 20," my school teacher announced with a big grin accompanied by curiosity. He took another concerned look at the script to confirm any mistake or mix up, but no, the result was mine. I stood from my seat, completely perplexed over the announcement. The shocking and displeasing look on the faces of my classmates didn't make things any easier either. It doubled my distress by 100%. In a matter of minutes, my heartbeat skyrocketed, and my head began to ache.

"Could this be a dream?" I asked myself.

Unfortunately, it wasn't. It slowly dawned on me that I had failed as I walked towards the front of the class to receive my English language test script. I recalled my teacher trying to say a few things, only by his lips' up and down movement, but I could not decode as little as a word he said, as my listening comprehension was far from me. Even the murmuring within the class sounded fuzzy. Everyone was surprised and disappointed. Almost every lip was moving.

"How did I go from one of the best to 4 out of 20 in a test?" I wondered. This was probably the same thing the entire class was talking about. I managed to collect the script from my teacher and walked back to my seat.

Did I play too much or took things for granted? How did I end up with such a disappointing result? I was so angry with myself. I didn't see any reason to blame anyone but myself. I just wanted the class to be over, so I could go home and nurse my pain. It's funny how the class ended with no one coming around to console me. Maybe my countenance didn't give room for that, or perhaps no one cared. While I was getting ready to leave, my closest friend walked up to me. I could have sworn that she came to console me, but no, she surprisingly made a jeering statement:

"Form Four will form fool you."

"Haba! on top of my situation Anty!" "Nothing wey Musa no go see for gate!" (Pidgin English slangs to communicating surprise and shock).

For the first time in my life, I felt lost and alone. The common saying about failure being an orphan and success having many siblings made complete sense to me.

Owing to the experience, I reviewed my friendships within and outside of school. I had to adequately separate my real friends from people who stood by while the success lasted. It took a while to recover from the blow and side talks, but with time things got better. I put in more work and effort, cut my leisure times, kept fewer friends to focus and do better, and I did do better. As a result, my grade improved to a 19 out of 20, and by the end of the term, my average was at 11.5 out of 20, translating to a pass mark on the subject.

I agree that this event brought me some level of distress I had not felt before that time. But truthfully speaking, the learning from this experience cut me deep. Firstly, the announcement came as a humbling shock and taught me that I am not failure-proof and could be abandoned. Secondly, the realisation that what counts is what I make out of a failure rather than what it does to me.

What does failure mean to me? And my answer is "forward." As the popular saying puts it "fail forward."

So failure to me means: falling, rising, and trying again; this time differently, until I reach my goal.

22
Lose the Battle, Win the War

"Excuse me, Ma'am, this subject is not for me; I am not willing to continue with it," I said with tears in my eyes as I ran behind my Form Four Additional Mathematics teacher at PCHS Kumbo, Cameroon. Her response was as direct as it could get; "if this is not for you, who then? If you talked less and focused more on this subject, maybe we wouldn't be having this conversation." Not satisfied with her response, I took it one step further to the Vice Principal (Academics). As I knocked and walked into his office, I didn't waste any seconds before letting him know why I was there. "Sir, I will like to drop Additional Mathematics." He looked at me calmly, said nothing for a few seconds and then responded with his usual fatherly voice. "Why would you want to do such?"

"I don't want any red marks (meant failed) on my report card," I replied.

"Is that all? If that's the only reason, you must report to me regularly to brief me on your progress in this subject. And finally, you have no other option than to pass the subject at the final exams. If you are worried that you will have a red ink in your report card, then make sure you don't fail the subject," he concluded. That was the end of the discussion.

I had gone to the Vice Principal's office that afternoon because he was in charge of subject registration and was responsible for approving my decision to quit Additional Mathematics. But I got more than I bargained! Going to him exposed me, and my willingness to drop a subject. His non-approval of my request meant I was basically on his radar. I felt he had given me an impossible responsibility by tasking me to ensure I passed the subject. To put this in a better perspective, at that point, we had written the two out of three tests that we usually had before the final exams. I had a 5/15 in the first test and a 6/20 in the second test giving me a total of 12.6/40. To have a pass mark on this subject meant that I needed at least 17.4/20 to average a 30/60, which was an apparent impossibility. What could be worse, the third test was to take place in two days!

I left his office more confused than I was when I bashed in with so much confidence just a few minutes earlier. As I headed to our dormitory, I was utterly clueless about achieving this impossible task that he had given me. I blamed myself for going to him in the first place. Why didn't I just let sleeping dog lie? I asked myself. He was a no-nonsense man, and the entire school knew too well not to be deceived by his calm demeanour and soft voice. You don't want to be in his bad book.

I had gone from "frying pan to fire." Obviously, I would fail the test, but this wasn't anymore the only disaster that was waiting to happen. Firstly, I will have red ink on my report card, which meant not being an "Honour Roll Student"; the first time such will happen after four years in the school. Secondly, I will have to explain myself to the Vice-Principal! But, what sent shivers down my spine and occupied most of my thoughts each time I remember explaining myself to him was the memory of the flogging he gave to one of my classmates. Oh dear, I can only wish and pray that such misfortune shouldn't befall me. How will I avert this oncoming disaster?

That night I realised the only way out of this predicted misfortune was to face this subject as my life depended on it; indeed, my life did. Since I struggled with the subject, I approach a senior colleague who was one of the best students in Form Five (a year ahead of me). I went to his dormitory that evening, and after explaining my situation to him, he agreed to help me out. My joy knew no bounds! We scheduled to meet after the evening preps at 9:00 pm. So after 9:00 pm that evening, we went to the dining hall, and he taught me through the various areas I was having challenges.

I felt my biggest challenge in grasping Additional Mathematics was a fundamental one since I was never a big fan of accepting things I didn't understand without a clear and convincing justification. His patience helped me in understanding the fundamentals I had challenges with. After the tutorial, we went back to the dormitory, but I couldn't just sleep since the test was scheduled for the following afternoon. I was perhaps the first to wake that morning and quickly headed to class to practice some more. That afternoon we had the test, and I must tell you I left the room feeling on top of the world. I couldn't imagine how I, of all people, answered all the questions in an Additional Mathematics test.

A few days later, the test results came out. I remember the teacher taking a long look at my script before calling out my name, Kelechukwu Onwukamike. I walked up to her with my heart beating like someone that had just completed a 100 meters sprint. She smiled as she handed me my script. When I looked at the score, I saw *14.5/15* and could not believe my eyes. This score translated to a 19.6/20, which was far above the 17.6/20 I needed to pass the subject. I had achieved the impossible! My classmates couldn't believe their eyes.

That evening I went to see the senior student that helped me and thanked him immensely; "I couldn't have done this without you," I said.

He looked at me, smiled and said, "where there is a will, there is always a way." The next day I walked majestically and proudly to the Vice-Principal's office to show my test score. While he was indeed very happy for me, my smiling face was an expression beyond passing the test but equally conveyed my joy of averting to sing the sad melodies induced by his flogging. I left his office more challenged to never give up because of short term benefits.

Eventually, I passed Additional Mathematics at the GCE O-level examination with a B-grade. This experience made me to deepen my interest in Mathematics. Thus, when I took the GCE A-level exams two years after, I had A-grades in both Advanced level Pure Mathematics and Further Mathematics. Mathematics became one of my favourite subjects that I even considered majoring in at the university.

However, it is important to remember that my love for Mathematics did not start from a place of comfort. I was about to quit Additional Mathematics because I was worried about the red mark on my report card!

Losing sight of the bigger picture because of the immediate benefit (being an Honour Roll student in my case) is not new to humankind. However, listening and being challenged by others than ourselves (in my case, the Vice-Principal Academics) could offer us the rare opportunity to leave our comfort zone so that we can win tomorrow.

I learnt from this experience that if you want it and are willing to put the work behind that dream, you can achieve it. Never forget that you can lose the battle, but this shouldn't discourage you from looking forward to the war, which is what counts. Each day we are faced with different types of challenges and failures, don't let this force you into short term thinking. The lessons from the failure you are experiencing might be all you need for the next big thing in your life.

THEME 7:
The Scholars Ship

23
Process over Result

"Please, can you mentor me towards winning a scholarship? I have been applying for many years but nothing to show for it," he said, sounding defeated. "What have you learnt from all these years?" I asked. "Being rejected for all scholarships I applied for, what is there to learn?" He replied.

As a mentor to many scholarship enthusiasts, I make it a point of note to remind them repeatedly what a scholarship is: an enabler of their vision but not their vision itself. Like this frustrated LinkedIn connection that reached out to me, many, including myself, at some point felt it was a waste of time with 'this scholarship thing'. And when you give your brain enough time to process such thoughts, the misconception that perhaps "scholarship is not for you" creeps in. Now I know better, and I'm usually very quick to remind my mentees to savour the process over the result. If you have been applying for scholarships for many years, the only way to keep your sanity, and of course not quit, is to let the process build you. Focusing on the outcome alone reduces all the effort you have exuded to nothing. The application process, the CV, the motivation letter/SOPs written, networking skills you have developed by reaching out to others to get help and the efforts you undertook to improve your chances are all worthy of commendation, don't forget.

Remember to celebrate small wins to keep your resilience and boost your motivation while on a scholarship quest. As researchers have repeatedly shown, taking a moment to celebrate any win (small or big) is a sure way to stay positive against all odds. Whereas there are various scholarships worldwide with different application processes, requirements and selection processes, taking a moment to celebrate getting through each stage will help keep you motivated. For example, completing your application before the deadline is not a small win. Realising the percentage of applicants that started but never completed will make you appreciate how amazing you are for completing yours. Also, putting yourself out there to compete with thousands of people worldwide is another remarkable feat that should make you feel proud. Be proud that your academic qualifications are considered worthy of international postgraduate positions. Yes, you might not have gotten funding, but you should appreciate the fact that you got to the interview stage. I agree that you might have been put on a waitlist and not the main list, but you should still celebrate the fact that you got to that stage. It is okay to be sad for not being selected, but don't stay sad and frustrated till the next application.

Just as with many aspects of life, we can approach our scholarship journey with a fixed or growth mindset. A fixed mindset sees rejection as the end of the road. When the application of people with such a mindset gets rejected, they take it as a personal rejection, not their application. Thus, they won't see any reason to improve themselves for subsequent application(s). When it's time for another application, they will hesitate to apply because they are afraid of getting another rejection. Thus, if they finally decide to apply, they start their application almost at the deadline. Since they didn't have enough time to prepare, they will apply with the previous year's background and experience level (copy and paste the past). Then, another rejection comes that will further frustrate and push them farther from ever applying again. Eventually, this group of people never wins any scholarship, not because they are inadequate, but because they have a fixed mindset that personalises rejection. Such a mindset preconditions people for serial failures.

On the other hand, those who approach the scholarship process with a growth mindset will receive the rejection and recognise that it is their application that was rejected and not them. They will take a step further to seek feedback on areas they can improve. They will take necessary proactive steps to close the gaps highlighted in their application feedback. They will apply the following year again with a much better application than the previous year. Even if they receive another rejection, they will recognise that "it is process over result" and won't fail to acknowledge how the process is helping them grow. They focus on improving themselves every time, and their application gets better each time because they do not feel that what they can know is "fixed"; instead, they keep improving. Also, because they keep doing it differently each time, eventually, they will win the scholarship. Even then, they are not quick to dismiss or forget the process that got them that result. The scholarship award doesn't cause them to become relaxed; instead, it pushes them further towards personal/intellectual development. The outcome is that they will perform exceptionally well in their graduate studies, further justifying that they were worthy of the scholarship award. In addition, with such brilliant performance, they increase their chances to succeed in the next phases of their life.

We can choose which category we want to fall in. Just as Dr Carol S. Dweck shared in her book, *Mindset, the New Psychology of Success*, no one is born with a growth or fixed mindset. Instead, they develop over time depending on how one deals with life experiences. When you see the scholarship journey as a process capable of building you up, you approach it differently. You will understand that being rejected from a scholarship doesn't mean you as a person have been rejected. Instead, you will seek feedback from the scholarship selection committee on areas you can improve to increase your chances. These areas become fertile grounds on which you develop and grow. As a result, your experience is broadened, and you become a better version of yourself.

"I work on their *mindset* because winning a scholarship starts in the mind. And anyone that wins in the mind will eventually win in reality; it becomes only a matter of time." This has always been my response anytime people ask me what I do differently in my mentorship platform that got 25 scholarship winners in 2020, 61 scholarship winners in 2021 and over 50 scholarship winners as of September 2022.

If you will ever have a chance or a shot at getting a scholarship, then only one thing is sure: '*Never Quit*'. Instead, let the process build and prepare you for that vision the scholarship can enable. While you work towards a successful scholarship application, make sure you are constantly improving - keep inching towards your goal.

24
Scholarship: For Me, Or Not For Me

When I got admitted to study Industrial Chemistry at the Federal University of Technology, Owerri, one of the first conversations I overheard was regarding the inferiority of Nigerian university certificates. This group of undergraduates I had just met at the SENATE building during a "validation exercise" didn't leave any stone unturned in down-casting the education they were about to receive. As far as they were concerned, studying in Nigeria was a waste of time.

Based on my experience, I understood later that having such a mindset was the first step to never getting a scholarship. When you are not confident in the quality of the education you have received, how can you be confident enough to put that certificate and your educational experience together and write a convincing motivation letter when competing for international scholarships? No one can believe in what you have to offer more than you. Therefore, we must not forget that winning a scholarship starts from the mind as captured in the preceding chapter.

In the past three years, over one hundred and thirty-five (135) of my mentees have gone on to win international scholarships. Their experiences and mental disposition that eventually got them the scholarship made me realise that the journey, challenge, and struggle are worth celebrating more than the scholarship itself. Why should they celebrate the process rather than the result, you might ask? From my experience, celebrating the process is more important because it is the process that birth results.

I must not fail to mention that I also went through the same phases and experiences during my scholarship quest. Arriving at the mindset of "process over results" did not come without the pains and disappointments. It was so challenging to clinch any scholarship that I felt 'this scholarship thing' is not for me.

Let me take this moment to share my scholarship journey as a response to one of the wish from my LinkedIn connection. My scholarship journey didn't start "internationally" as many would imagine, but locally while as an undergraduate student in Nigeria.

I was part of various applications for undergraduate scholarships, being first shortlisted for the Shell Scholarship. The assessment took place in Enugu. Unfortunately, I didn't see the list of those that won that scholarship to date! This experience was followed by the first edition of the MTN Foundation Scholarship, in which I was shortlisted and eventually scaled through the assessment stage. A few weeks after the assessment, I was summoned by the secretary to our Head of Department, who informed me that MTN had sent a letter to the department to verify my results. Sadly, they dropped me at the end of the day since I used my second-year results (my first in the university) instead of year one results (which I did not have as I got admitted as a direct entry candidate). This experience was the closest I ever came to winning a scholarship. When the final list of successful candidates was released, I cried my eyes out. At that instance, I felt that scholarship was not for me, and I should not pursue it any further. Hence, I stopped applying to all undergraduate scholarships and focused on my studies.

While I did not receive any undergraduate scholarship, it would be unfair if I failed to mention the 10,000 naira (about 60$) worth scholarship awarded to me by the Enugu state branch of my town union. I had to spend about 2,500 naira and travel from Owerri to Enugu to receive this award. In all earnest, this was my very first scholarship.

Having decided to focus on my studies and leave the *scholarship thing,* in my third year, my older brother won the prestigious Erasmus Mundus scholarship for a double master program between the UK and Germany. At that point, I did not know the value of the scholarship, but I remembered that he resigned from his job at Procter & Gamble, Ibadan, for this scholarship. When I visited to bid him farewell, he shared the value of the scholarship, 40,000 euros! I was dumbfounded! So a Nigerian education and certificate can make someone competitive enough to win such a scholarship? This question kept running through my mind. Would you blame me? Remember the earlier experience I shared about the undergraduate students I met on arriving in FUTO.

I felt proud of my brother. This experience rekindled my hope in the possibility of winning a scholarship someday.

There is no doubt that my brother winning such a prestigious scholarship was a turning point regarding my impression of scholarships in general. Moreover, by sharing a similar background with him as a graduate of FUTO, I ruled out the bias that was beginning to grow regarding the inferiority of Nigerian university certificates.

I made my first international scholarship application one year after my brother left for Europe with this renewed energy.

I owe the completion of this first application to him, who made sure I didn't rest till it was submitted. He had sent the link to the Erasmus Mundus programs and asked that I apply to three that best fit my interest. I had only part of my results at this point as I was still in my fourth year for a five-year degree program. When I mentioned that my results were incomplete, he wouldn't have it and insisted that I apply with what I have. He guided me on how to prepare a self-student unofficial transcript. Later, I had to deal with the constraint of not possessing an international passport yet. He insisted that I apply with my student ID and explain to the selection board that I would get an international passport before commencement if selected. For every excuse I could have come up with, my older brother found a way to give me an alternative. Finally, I ran out of excuses and decided to apply.

The process was indeed very challenging, as my brother was not the type of coach that will hold your hand all the way, you had to learn it the hard way and only when you have drafted your motivation letter or statement of purpose (SOPs) that he will give it a look. So finally, I applied for three Erasmus

Mundus programs. I remember the IMETE (The International Master of Science in Environmental Technology and Engineering) program very well because I also needed to post certified hard copies of my documents for this application. I remember how I was charged 2,500 naira for each notary stamp and how I went to the NIPOST office in Lagos on the 23rd of December 2010 to post the documents since this was the cheapest option. The application was received two weeks after the deadline. Still, luck came through for me as I had written to the selection coordinator that I posted the mail before the deadline, stating how the delay was not within my power, and they accepted. So in my first year of application, I got "three love letters", with the usual reason for rejection being that so many suitable applications were received with only limited funding available.

As much as I did not get any of the scholarships I applied for, the experience helped me get familiar with the application process. In addition, I felt excited that even as an undergraduate, the selection committee took the time to go through my application and made a decision.

In the following year, then as a final year undergraduate student, I made my second scholarship application. I was more prepared than the previous year, having obtained most of the requirements. As an example, I took my TOEFL exam, in which I scored 95/120. In addition, my international passport was ready. The application process was very stressful as I had to submit hard copy applications by post. My only option for sending these hard copy applications was to use the cheapest posting service (NIPOST), which costed 1,000 naira for Europe compared to DHL that charged 15,000 naira. While trying to meet deadlines, I completed my applications much earlier to account for the two weeks delivery time. After the applications, I earnestly awaited their outcomes. Then, the results started dropping in and finally I was given a place on one of the programmes on self-funding (IMETE). The other two were not successful. Since I could not afford the self-funding offer, I had to decline.

Outside of applying to Erasmus Mundus scholarships during my scholarship hunting, I also started sending emails to Professors in Canada, USA and Australia. My strategy was to search for professors in the field of study closest to what I intended to do in graduate school. During this time, I sent well over one hundred emails and got only one response that year.

My third year of applying for international scholarships was in 2012. Then, I just graduated from university and was mobilised for National Youth Service Corps (NYSC). Amongst the three programs under the Erasmus Mundus Scholarship that I applied was FAME (Functionalised Advanced Materials and Engineering). This program was not initially on my list of selected options but was brought to my notice by my older brother when he visited Nigeria after completing his Erasmus Mundus program. He felt that since the FAME program was focused on material science, it was the best fit for me as an Industrial Chemistry graduate. He was right because I completely fell in love with the program when I went through the course modules.

I made the application and forgot about it until one fateful morning in February 2013. At this point, I was almost rounding up with my youth service in Port Harcourt, Nigeria, when I received an email that I had been shortlisted for an interview for the Erasmus Mundus FAME master program. I felt like screaming, and indeed I screamed! I could not believe my eyes. I checked the email repeatedly to be sure it was not some prank. I was asked to choose the most suitable time for my interview. I selected the closest date as I didn't want to take any chances.

The day of the interview came, and precisely at 4:00 pm, my phone rang. The interview commenced with professors from Grenoble Alps, France. The focus was on material physics, with questions on conductors, semiconductors, silicon materials and the likes. Funny enough, I didn't prepare specifically for these questions but responded favourably due to my knowledge in this area from my high school Physics. Furthermore, responding to these questions simply because of my previous studies years ago justified my usual approach of studying to understand and not just to pass an exam. I might have missed a few points, but I felt grateful to have progressed to that stage.

About two weeks later, I got an email that I was among the top candidates on the reserved list. I remember sharing the news with a friend who was very confident that I would get the scholarship. Then The following week, I was nominated for another scholarship. The AMADEUs LabEx (Advanced Materials by Design Laboratory of Excellence) scholarship that could cover my cost to participate in the program. This scholarship was offered by the University of Bordeaux, France, one of the partner universities in the FAME Masters consortium. However, it wasn't an automatic scholarship as I needed to go through another round of interviews.

I had resumed as a Graduate Assistant in the Chemistry Department, Federal University of Technology, Owerri, within the same period I was scheduled for the scholarship interview. Out of the fear that I might have issues with my internet (it was supposed to be a Skype interview), I ensured my laptop was well charged and bought sufficient data. However, I lost the internet connection in the staff office I had set up for my interview, just as I feared. So I had to carry my laptop and walked around the campus until I got an internet network under a tree. When I finally connected, the first comment I made to the professors from the University of Bordeaux was how I had to stay under a tree to have the interview. The interview was majorly on Material Chemistry which made all the sense since both professors were in the Chemistry institute. The questions covered areas on thermodynamics, entropy and so on.

After the interview, checking my emails became an addiction. I will check almost every 10 minutes. But it was after a week that my "one yes" email finally dropped in at past 9:00 pm. "We are happy to inform you that you have been selected for the AMADEUs LabEx Scholarship worth eighteen thousand euros (€18,000) for two years to participate in the Erasmus Mundus FAME program." I was transfixed on my screen. I couldn't believe my eyes; my heart was beating so fast that I felt I was going to faint. So this was it? Finally, I got an international scholarship. I couldn't contain the thrills of excitement as I hastily accepted the offer before the day came to an end. I recall asking myself so many rhetorical questions, "so this scholarship thing can also be for me?"

"Kelechukwu, this is it!" I affirmed, and this was how my international scholarship journey to Europe started.

25
After The One Yes

Finally, the long-awaited results arrived. Having ploughed, persisted, did it differently, the long-expected "one yes" arrived. But, in our celebratory mood, we forget what comes after.

In my case, acquiring an international scholarship was all that mattered. Before being awarded a scholarship, getting it was not just the main thing but the "ONLY THING". I thought that everything else would fall in place once granted, and I would walk on the red carpet to my scholarship destination. Unfortunately, I failed to realise that with success comes more challenges to sustain the success.

After receiving the notification of my scholarship, the first challenge occurred after I got my visa appointment date at the German embassy in Lagos, Nigeria. At this point, I was waiting for the official scholarship letter to be mailed to me. Three days before my interview appointment, I woke up to discover my laptop and phone had been stolen during the night while I was sleeping. Thieves broke into my room at the university and carted away my phone and laptop. I was in shock, "what am I going to do?" I kept asking myself.

Just as I stepped out of the room in the quest to figure out what to do next, I noticed a tiny object lying on the floor. It was my sim card, dropped just in front of the building. I quickly placed the sim card into an available phone, and right after, a call came in. It was from the DHL courier service in Enugu; they had a parcel for me and couldn't locate the address I had provided. Finally, I was able to get their location for the pickup in Enugu. When I dropped the call, I couldn't begin to imagine how bad this could have been if I did not find my sim card. This would have hindered me from fulfilling the requirements needed to attend my visa interview. There would have been no visa and scholarship.

This incident taught me that when things seem to be going all bad, we should take a step back and appreciate where we are because it could even be worse.

If I thought this was the worst that could happen while preparing for my trip to Germany, I was not paying attention. After attending the visa interview in Lagos, I went back to the Federal University of Technology Owerri, where I was already a Graduate Assistant. After a week, my access to my yahoo email was denied. Till date, I am yet to figure out what went wrong. All I remember was that I could not access my Yahoo email account. Then came the struggle, my friend and I explored all methods to access my email, but all were in vain.

At this time, I was expecting a response from the German embassy regarding the decision on my visa. One week passed, and still, I could not access my email. What made it worse was that I had no phone or a laptop. This meant I had to trek few kilometers from my house to the university campus to use a desktop at the public café. Each day, after exhausting the number of attempts at recovering my password, I would return home and try the next day, hoping to be successful. One of the security questions to which I could not recall the response was, "who is your favourite uncle?" After exhausting all the possible names that I could remember, the whole process was futile. I decided to reach out to my older brother, who had created my Yahoo email aacount ten years earlier. I hoped perhaps he would remember the answer we used for this question. Sadly, all suggestions he made were unsuccessful. I was drenched in sadness.

The second week came through, yet no positive outcome. At this point, I was losing a grip of myself and could no longer contain the stress and chaos. I wondered why I had to go through such mental torture because I got a scholarship. My worries only got worse because I did not know if the German consulate had made the visa decision. Was I supposed to pick the visa within a specific time? I had no idea.

My resumption was fast approaching which only went further to compound my woes. At this point, I felt everything was working against me and were moving in the opposite direction.

I kept asking myself if I should abandon the scholarship to enjoy peace of mind.

At the end of the second week of trying to resolve my Yahoo email access problem, I was wandering around the university campus when I felt an urge to pray in my heart.

"Lord Jesus, help me, for I do not know what else to do," I prayed.

Just then, it felt like I heard the name "Johnson." Johnson, Johnson, who is Johnson? I struggled to recall after what seemed an eternity, "*Oh, boy,*" I jumped in excitement as I remembered that Johnson was one of my uncles. However, he was not on my favourite uncles list. I don't know how his name made it to my Yahoo email account as my most favourite uncle.

Without any waste of time, I ran back to the cybercafé and entered the name "Johnson" when I was prompted by Yahoo mail to enter my "favourite uncle's name."

My hands, legs and every part of my body were shaking when I entered the name. Then, boom! It went through. I had access to my Yahoo email account. I jumped and screamed to the surprise of everyone that was in the cybercafé that moment.

Those two weeks of constant mental torture made me realise that we take many things for granted, such as accessing our emails account and quickly forget their actual worth. This was one of those times that I appreciated that the simplest of tasks could soon become the most critical and pivotal to everything else in our lives.

I quickly went to my inbox to see if the German embassy had sent any email. But there was none; I sighed and heaved while settling back to my seat. So have I been worried all this while for nothing? I asked myself. Then another thought came to check my spam. I wondered why the email could even be in the spam in the first place—considering that I had received an email from the German embassy in my inbox in the past.

What was there to lose anyway? So I checked my spam folder. And there it was!

"Oh my God!" I exclaimed. They had sent it a week ago! My heart started beating very fast as I opened the email, fearing the worst, which could be that the collection date had passed. I remember observing during my visa interview appointment how the security officials at the German consulate, Lagos treated applicants coming to the consulate and how strict they were with appointment times and dates. I was apprehensive because I had no clue what to do if my collection date had passed. However, when I finally opened the email, it turned out different, and I could come for pick up on any working day with my email printout.

The next day I left for Lagos and without any further drama was able to collect my passport with my Germany visa already stamped in it. My trip to Germany gradually became a reality. But there was still yet another obstacle.

The challenge of raising funds required for paying my flight ticket and accommodation rent for the first month became a sting. And after exhausting all available banks who offered loans at ridiculous interest rates, my older brother saved me from their hands & sponsored my trip in full.

When I finally got to Germany on the 30th of September 2013, I knew clearly in my heart that this journey had just begun.

My experience showed clearly that once we conquer one battle, challenge, or failure, we live to fight or face another one.

The overall experiences I had after my "one yes" fits nicely into my ideology of "we are always a work in progress." In the real sense of this statement, there will always be something to work on, learn, unlearn, and relearn; we need to stay alert.

When you get that "one yes" email you have been waiting for all these years, don't fail to get prepared for the journey that comes after. Do not feel discouraged or heartbroken; when these challenges start popping up. Remember that, "diamonds are made under heat and pressure."

26
Writing It Down: What I Did Differently As a Student

"KC, tell us what you did differently as a student?" "How did you manage to accumulate all these awards and achievements within such a short time?" These were among the questions my LinkedIn connection wanted me to cover in this book. In this chapter, I will try to do justice to these questions.

It might be difficult to point to the "one thing" that I did that differentiated me from my peers. However, I can confidently say that my "summary notes" contributed significantly to my achievements. I recently came across the summary notes of all courses I took during my double MSc degree program. However, this habit didn't start during my master program but over twenty years ago.

You might be puzzled to ask, what could have led me to develop this habit in the first place? Also, you might want to know how this habit has helped differentiate me from my peers? So let me share in the following paragraphs.

When I was about ten years old, one of my class teachers advised us to write down anything we wanted to remember. His advice stuck in my mind, and from that day onwards, I created what I called "summary notes" for all the subjects I took. This habit became my lifestyle and played a pivotal role in positioning me at the top in the presence of very brilliant classmates. Graduating top in the A-level GCE was the first time a non-Cameroonian achieved such a feat in my school.

When I got admitted to study Industrial Chemistry at the Federal University of Technology Owerri, this habit stayed with me. Eventually, I graduated with First-Class Honours as the best graduating student of the department and Faculty of Sciences. Those who know this university will agree that making a first-class from Industrial Chemistry is near impossible. As you might recall, as I earlier shared, when I got newly admitted, I was told to forget about graduating with a First class.

Is this habit implementable outside the shore of our home country? You might wonder. My response to that is a resounding "Yes." This same habit was instrumental to how I ended up as one of the best graduating students from the Erasmus Mundus FAME master program that was done in Germany and France.

The reapplication of this technique has been proven times without number. When I shared it with some of my undergraduate classmates, the outcomes were astonishing. Most of them performed far better in courses/subjects where this technique was applied.

Now that I have shared the "secret" to my success, you might want to know how I managed to be consistent in applying this technique and how I went about it. In addition, what tips could I share for anyone who would like to consider this technique?

I noticed earlier that summarising (compressing) my notes made them very handy to carry around and easier to read through repeatedly. Secondly, these summary notes were written by me in a way that I could understand what the professor had taught, so it was faster to comprehend than my lectures' notes. The most challenging part was making the summary due to the bulky lecture notes. To avoid this, I tried as much as possible to summarise immediately after every lecture, and when this was not possible, I did well to summarise before the next lecture.

Therefore, the first step is usually to create a study timetable. Typically, I waited till I had the school timetable before preparing mine; in this way, I could align both. This structure of my reading timetable helped ensure that I summarised the notes after every lecture. Since I didn't rely only on my lectures, I usually had to create a separate reading timetable that allocated time for me to study recommended texts and other materials and equally summarise them. By summarising my notes, I could easily identify what is not clear to me and quickly address them.

How did I tackle my examinations?

At the start of every semester, I would ensure that I had pasted my desired results on my reading table. Almost everyone who walked into my room would have caught a glance at it. I usually asked myself one question: "What would be my reason for not making the best grade (A on the Nigerian scale or 1.0 on a German scale)?" The answer to this question was what I called the "gap", which needed to be closed to achieve the best grade. Once I had identified this gaps, I paid more attention to getting them addressed. Closing these identified gaps ranged from studying more to seeking help from someone who understood better that course or subject.

I hope this chapter has done justice to the question on what I did differently as a student.

I also hope those who apply this technique will get even more significant benefits than I did. As usual, nothing gives me greater joy than seeing people succeed in their endeavours.

THEME 8:
Direction over Speed

27
No Rush: The Danger of Frustration Induced Decision

When I completed my high school in Cameroon, where I graduated as the best student, I returned to Nigeria in the third quarter of 2007. The next step for my education was to commence undergraduate studies. My older brother had assisted me in applying for a direct entry to the Federal University of Technology Owerri. A direct entry admission meant I would commence from the second year in the university instead of the first year. Considering that my A-level GCE certificate was the requirement for such a direct entry, I was very confident that getting admission would be a piece of cake.

Fast forward to early January 2008, I had no admission, and my waiting patience was finally wearing thin. My dad had recommended that I register and sit for the general Nigerian university entry examination called JAMB, which was in my opinion, far below my standard. For crying out loud, I was two years long past that level, I said to myself and refused to register when it was first proposed. It's been a month since my dad had first made this suggestion, and the deadline for this examination registration was fast approaching, yet no admission for me. During this same period, my classmates from Cameroon had already resumed their university education as of September 2007. The more I thought about it, the more frustrated I became. When I saw that failing to register for the JAMB examination would mean not only staying at home for a year but at least two, I gave in to my dad's pressure and registered for the exam. The thought of staying at home for one year (time from writing the exam to when a potential admission will be given), left me a very sad person. Before finding myself in this melancholy, I had a smooth education ride, and not once was I out of school except during public school holidays. And now, see me; Kelechukwu, the best graduating student from my high school, will now stay at home for a year. No way.

So on that fateful morning, I paced around our village home, a routine I had started the previous week to help calm my nerves with the tiniest thing enough to trigger an outburst. My dad walked up to me with a Daily Newspaper in hand.

"K-boy," he called out, a way to soothe me as he was the one who was watching his son go from the usual bubbling boy to a reclusive and sad person. Please don't blame *me o*, that's how much I like school.

I turned around to see my dad beaming with his usual smile. What could be making him so happy? I wondered. In fact, for a split second, I thought he might have received the news of my admission. But that was not the case. He had seen an advert for a part-time degree program at the University of

Benin, Nigeria, and felt it would be an option for me instead of staying at home. I jumped at it without a second thought and quickly planned to travel to Benin the following week.

En route Benin, I passed through Enugu, where my older sister was living at the time. When we talked, I shared my plan for the part-time program with her. "Let me see the advert you are talking about," she said. I handed it over to her, and she buried her head in it, taking all the time to digest the information on the advert. After what seemed like an eternity, she looked up and spoke to me as direct as she could ever be.

"KK, you are so young (I was 20 years old then) and very smart, part-time is for working-class and older people," "Please, for your future sake, don't take this route, you will be more frustrated," she advised. It was not easy to let go, but my sister has always loved me, and I was convinced she knew better and had my interest at heart. This was how my trip to Benin ended.

When I look back, I can't but thank God I listened to her and did not go ahead with my decision, which was born out of desperation and frustration.

Two weeks after letting go of the part-time program, I got a full-time direct entry admission to study Industrial Chemistry at the Federal University of Technology Owerri (FUTO), thereby starting from the second year.

My stay in FUTO became a solid foundation on which everything else I built stood. This success included breaking the long jinx in the Chemistry department by graduating with a First Class and being among the very first set to receive my appointment and resume as a Graduate Assistant less than one month after my youth service in 2013.

The fun fact from this experience was that I went ahead to take the JAMB exam since I had registered for it before getting admitted into my degree program at FUTO. Although I got an impressive score of 298/400, the result was withheld for reasons still unknown to me to date! In time past and now, I have come to express great admiration for Nigerians that wrote this examination and got admitted into the university without the kind of drama I had.

This experience helped me understand the importance of being patient by acknowledging our unique path and destiny. We must not feel the pressure to do everything possible simply because we want to catch up with our peers. As we all know, in every race, the winner is not usually the person who led first but the one who ended first.

If we fail to have the foresight and look beyond the obvious of what is available, we might get entrapped in our choice and lose many years trying to find our way out.

Frustration, disappointments, and failures will come in this sojourn of life. So be on the lookout not to rush into every available "opportunity," for they might be a trap and killer of time, and by "rushing to meet up," we are more exposed to be a prey to our frustration-induced decision.

No two people have the same destiny, and you are not late because your mates have graduated, got married, got jobs, while you are still looking for all these.

Run your race, your time will come.

28
Not What I Am Looking For: I Am Not Studying Industrial Chemistry

Generally, I do not accept things just because that's how they are. This trait has often led to being labelled stubborn or a rebel. This aspect of me came into play on that evening in late January 2008 when my dad informed me that I had been admitted into the Federal University of Technology Owerri (FUTO). Of course, he expected it would be a cause for celebration. However, how I reacted upon receiving the news shocked my dad, he didn't see that coming. You would remember how my dad watched me grow frustrated with each passing day due to the delay of my admission into the university?

So when he informed me of my admission, instead of jumping at it, I asked a question, "which course?" I recalled him mentioning Industrial Chemistry.

"Hold on dad," I said to him with a dubious tone. "Did you just say Industrial Chemistry?"

"Yes son, it doesn't matter which course it is; what's paramount is that you got an admission." He replied.

"But Dad," as I looked at him with a sad face, "you don't understand."

My dad naturally gets riled very easily. He wasted no time and reprimanded me on the spot. Little did he know that I actually wanted to do an engineering course and had already envisioned myself as a future engineer. Studying engineering was on the vision board that I had created many years prior. I suddenly became emotional and couldn't fathom that I'd be stuck doing something in pure science; this was not what I wanted! Quite frankly, if I had wanted to do something related to pure science, I would have opted for Mathematics due to my strong interest in the subject!

Saying my dad was shocked at my reaction would be an understatement.

Was I not the same person that paced round our village compound crying like a lost sheep for not getting an admission? Was I not the same person that came very close to enrolling for a part-time program at the University of Benin, Nigeria, till my older sister convinced me out of it?

He wondered how I could not be happy about getting the much-sought-after admission but more worried about what offered course?

When my dad noticed he could not convince me otherwise, he called my older brother. Remember, he has always been my mentor, so he articulated and shared his pearls of wisdom in educating me about the possibilities of Industrial Chemistry.

Finally, after two hours of deliberating and reasoning, I let my guard down and had a change of perspective.

Nonetheless, we both decided that I must give Industrial Chemistry a chance and later switch to Chemical or Petroleum Engineering after my first year. Why didn't I think of this before? I guess my head was too fixated on engineering; hence I didn't want to open a room for pure science.

This option to switch from Industrial Chemistry to Chemical engineering was good news. There is a cause to celebrate, after all. But, long story short, after spending just one year studying Industrial Chemistry, I couldn't love the course any less and stayed till the very end.

Looking back at those days, I laugh at my sheer ignorance of what Chemistry could offer. I had no idea what it was about since, as a kid, we grew up with one future aspiration; be a doctor, an engineer, or a lawyer. However, it was already clear from secondary school that I had phobia for blood. So, this left me with one option - Engineering.

These titles stuck with us without necessarily understanding and realising the vast opportunities in other fields of study. The truth is, I never knew what I was looking for. I just wanted to be called an engineer! However, going through Industrial Chemistry opened my eyes to the vast possibilities available to people with such a background. Today, I have completed a double MSc in Material Science and Engineering focusing on Polymer Chemistry and equally completed a double PhD in Polymer and Organic Chemistry. If you had told the 20-year-old me in 2008 that I would not only fall in love with Chemistry, a course that I was so hesitant to take, but will go on to have a PhD in it twelve years later, I would have laughed it off as the joke of the century.

Life is about figuring things out as they come. Some might be clear a bit earlier. However, for others, we only know when we are already in it. And our newly found knowledge can lead us to our next phase of life. It is, therefore, very pertinent that we do well to organise various outreach events to secondary schools and even primary schools to educate them on other interesting fields besides law, engineering, and medicine. I firmly believe this will give these young students the correct orientation towards their future goals. Taking such sensitisation to the secondary school prompted DEKEMP to create "DEKEMP @ Secondary Schools Club." The focus of this club is to carry out sensitisation and awareness outreaches to secondary schools in our local vicinities.

THEME 9:
Seize the moment

29
What Is In Your Hand?

The Israelites were stranded.

Behind them, the fierce Egyptians were advancing.

Before them, the Red sea stood.

Moses waited for a miracle; perhaps God would send angels to save them.

What did God do? He asked Moses, "what do thou haveth in thy hand?"

"A staff," he replied.

"Then use it," God said.

The rest of the story is found in the Holy Bible, Exodus 14.

Before reaching without, take a moment to search within!

An African proverb says when suffering knocks on the door, and you say there is no seat for him, he tells you not to worry because he has brought his seat. How about we turn this around to sound like, "when opportunity tells you there is no seat for you, remind it that you've brought yours." At every point in life, opportunities lurk around waiting not only for those who identify with it but for those who will seize the moment and make it theirs.

This knowledge came well into play in 2018 when I attended a conference in New York City, USA. At this point, I was almost at the end of my PhD and was already looking for post-doctoral opportunities.

Knowing that I will be meeting a lot of key stakeholders in my area of research, I made sure to be well prepared for the conference. The first thing I did was make a poster that summarised all the work I had done, including the link to my published articles. I printed this poster on A4 papers, and this became my business card, which I intended to share with those I met. This poster flier proved to be very effective because even though I was to deliver an oral instead of a poster presentation, I could catch the interest of many of the big names in the field of renewable polymers. With this flier, I was able to gain their interest to attend my presentation scheduled on the third day. My talk took place in the morning following the conference dinner and was therefore not the best time to expect large attendance. I was gradually setting the stage for my big announcement, unknown to the big names I had earlier invited to my talk.

The day of my presentation arrived, and the hall was filled to the brim. Apparently, my campaigns had paid off. After delivering my presentation, I paused at the end and made an announcement: "I want to thank you all for attending my talk this morning despite the busy dinner last evening. I would like to use this opportunity to announce that I am rounding up my

PhD by early February 2019 and will be available for any opportunity that you may have or know someone that does." There was a good reaction from the audience with many clapping. After my presentation, I was approached by three different professors. In fact, one of the leading researchers in the field who had come from China made me an offer on the spot, "come to China for postdoc and I will pay you 50,000 USD after tax." I was also asked to submit a CV for a postdoc position in Canada and another in the USA. I also got great feedback from many of the professors in attendance who commended me for leveraging the stage I was given to advance my course. I left the conference that day, not only well known by many top names in my field but equally got some excellent offers to consider.

The learning here is always to think ahead, develop the ability to identify potential opportunities and seize the moment when it comes. It might be unconventional or unfamiliar, but who says unconventional is bad. The ability to seize opportunities rests on how self-conscious and aware we are of our environment; paying attention to details cannot be overemphasised.

Always remember to exploit your point of differentiation to your benefit. There is no one way to succeed, but by consistently evaluating and assessing your position and learning from your experience, you increase your odds. In shooting your shots, always rebuke the thought of what could go wrong.

Remember that before looking without, first look within for what you are looking for most times is within you.

So I ask you today, what is in your hand?

30
Brain Gain, Not Brain Drain

Sometime in 2021, I was privileged to be interviewed by *Vanguard Newspaper* Nigeria. During the interview, I was asked if I didn't think that promoting and mentoring Nigerian´s best students to travel out for their graduate studies abroad was contributing to the brain drain that the country had been experiencing over the years. This was not the first time I had been asked such a question that I considered very valid. It makes sense when you think that most of these international scholarships are very competitive, meaning most Nigerian or African students selected are among the best of their respective countries. Also, when we look at the low likelihood that any of them would return to their country of origin after completing their studies, it all adds up to the "brain drain" fear.

"It is not a brain drain but rather a brain gain." This has always been my response to this question.

Why do I call it brain gain?

My reason for seeing this as a brain gain is that when most brilliant students leave the shores of their home countries for graduate studies, they do so with a knowledge gap that needs to be filled to equip them best to contribute to their society adequately. Without gaining such international scholarships, their financial constraint will not allow them to get such an education.

A perfect example is the viral story of a Nigerian first-class Mathematics student who couldn't save the required funds to sponsor himself for international examinations such as General Record Examinations (GRE) and IELTS (International English Language Test Score) that would enable him to meet requirements to apply for graduate schools in the USA. This financial constraint held back this brilliant guy who resorted to teaching in a secondary school. Fortune shined on him when he was selected for the Michael Taiwo scholarship that helped fund his international exams, coached and mentored him towards graduate school admission. Eventually, he got a fully-funded PhD in the USA and currently studies in the USA. Let us imagine how his capabilities will be developed and sharpened during his PhD studies. Now compare his value to Nigerian society before and after the knowledge acquired during his postgraduate studies? At what point can we say he is more valuable to his society?

It is one thing to have potentials, but those that are not sharpened and enabled don't help much.

There is another dimension of what brain gain truly means for the technology savvy Africans who cannot utilize their skills to the maximum due to the constraint placed on them by their country of origin. This constraint could range from inadequate infrastructure to the absence of government support. One example that occurred in 2021 was a Nigerian youngster who developed drone prototypes from scratch. He repeatedly failed to get government support to further develop his ideas. Guess where he is today? Finland! I have a mentee who builds aeroplane models from scratch using available scrap materials. Once more, he is yet to get the necessary government support in terms of funding and integration into a system that can benefit his home country. Very soon, he too will be gone. We can now ask the question, without moving away to another country where their skills and talents are appreciated and rewarded, how can they use their God-given *brain* to truly make a difference? They will only get frustrated if such a critical move is not made because the environment they were born into doesn't provide the necessary support needed to make a valuable contribution to their society.

In my opinion, the benefit of the "brain" of such brilliant folks is not limited to their country of residence. What counts is how many Nigerians or Africans have received the proper training and developed their technical know-how. Maybe tomorrow, they might choose to relocate to their country of origin to lead from the "ground zero", but they could equally lead such an innovation revolution from their foreign base. A perfect example would be Prof. Ndubuisi Ekekwe, who resides in the USA. Nevertheless, he has spearheaded and brought his technical mastery to enable many start-ups in Africa, Nigeria in particular, and to be precise, Abia, his state of origin.

I used to think that I could only make a difference in my country by living there; today, that's not the case. Thousands of miles away, my little contributions towards human capacity development in Africa and Nigeria, in particular, are being felt.

It is equally from my abroad location that I gave a lecture on "research design and innovative methods" to PhD candidates at the African Centre of Excellence for Future Energies and Electrochemical Systems (ACE-FUELS), FUTO chapter. Could I have been able to deliver such a lecture eight years ago when I completed my undergraduate degree? The answer is "NO". Did the students learn less because they were being taught remotely? Again, the answer is no, as seen from the very positive feedback they gave.

This is what brain gain means; being able to develop the capability of your population. But, unfortunately, considering the thousands of brilliant graduate students seeking the opportunity to close the necessary gap that will allow them to make significant contributions to their society, many governments are just not able to fund their studies abroad. This is where international scholarships have stepped in.

In the end, the countries from which these brilliant students have left are not losing any brain, simply because the location has changed. In reality, and as an example, if we look at the billions of dollars that Nigerians in the diaspora remit back home every year, we can agree that beyond using their brain to work abroad to support their families home, many of these brains still extend a hand to provide solutions to contribute to the growth of their society.

This is what brain gain entails.

THEME 10:
Hope; the reason for tomorrow

31
Now or Later: Adapting & Thriving In a New Environment

How did you manage to adapt and thrive in new environments? This question was among those my LinkedIn connection wanted me to cover in this book.

As the readers might have known by now, I am originally Nigerian but born in Cameroon, which indicates that I was "born adapting."

I have so many lovely memories growing up in Cameroon. Notwithstanding, I became aware and lived with the consciousness that I was a foreigner from age ten/eleven. By the age of thirteen, I experienced my first and last arrest to date by the police. The detail of this encounter has been covered in an earlier chapter of this book.

Back to the discussion question, how did I adapt and thrive in such an environment?

Kindness: Thanks to my mum who taught my siblings and me to repay unfairness with kindness, I was able to fall back to this approach as a way of dealing with discriminatory experiences while growing up in Cameroon.

Self-acceptance: Kindness played a pivotal role in how I managed to keep my "cool" during unpleasant experiences. What I gradually realised was that accepting who I was; a foreigner, was very helpful. Sad, I know, and up to date, I still question myself if this was the best approach but sincerely it helped a great deal.

With this *self-acceptance*, all the name callings from my peers didn't matter to me. When my teachers sometimes made jokes about how complicated my name sounded, being a foreigner in class, I developed tough skin and focused on my school purpose. *Self-acceptance* gradually became the thick skin that I created to utilise my energy in what mattered to me; which was studying. Eventually, I graduated as the school's best student for all the qualification exams, starting from Ordinary & Advanced level GCE examinations.

All-win approach: during my time in Cameroon, I experimented with the group study approach to promote a collective win. I was able to develop solid relationships with Cameroon classmates through this effort, many of which have lived up to date. This played a massive role in helping me adapt and thrive in Cameroon despite how challenging the environment was.

After high school, I returned to my home country of Nigeria to resume my university undergraduate studies. If I thought this would take away the feeling of being a foreigner, I was wrong. I became "that Cameroon boy" because of the influence of the local Cameroonian dialect on both my English and native Igbo language. In addition, I met an environment steeped in competition. Here, the mentality of many people was how they can "out-do" or "out-smart" each other. I gradually became *"ewu Cameroon,"* which translates literally to "Cameroon goat" or someone who is not smart enough. This new name-calling was the outcome each time I tried to consider the interest of others while making my own choices.

How did I adapt to such an environment?

Not competition: first, I clarified that I was not there for a competition but to become the better version of myself through knowledge acquisition.

Birds of the same feather: what did they say birds of the same feather did? They flock together, *abi*? I quickly identified classmates who shared a similar mindset, and they equally helped me blend into the "Nigerian environment."

Lifting others: during my undergraduate studies, I employed the highly successful all-win approach I had developed while studying in Cameroon. This way, I helped my classmates by organising tutorials and personal lessons. This extra support I provided enabled me to fit perfectly into the group. In addition, I understood and retained my lectures better by teaching others.

After completing my undergraduate studies, I got a scholarship for my postgraduate studies in Europe, and another adaptation was needed.

On that morning of 30th September 2013, I walked out of Munich international airport and was entirely surrounded by people who didn't look like me for the first time in my life. I was shocked and instantly welcomed by the cold weather. This was one of those times that I felt alone in a very far land—the question of how I would survive engulfed my mind.

As I resumed my master's lectures at the University of Augsburg, I quickly noticed that I had to adapt not only to the cultural differences and weather, but also their teaching style. After my first lecture, I started wondering if I could follow the fast pace of the lecturers.

As a very picky eater, it was challenging to adapt to the food; I couldn't break the jinx within the first two years. I remember being the last person to order after spending so much time and still ending up with fries.

So with all these rather intimidating realities, how did I adapt during my first time in Europe and equally graduated among the best students of my master's studies?

Positive reaffirmation: this became my first strategy. When the going got tough, I would look into the mirror and positively reaffirm that, "I can do all things through Christ who gives me strength," (Philippians 4:13).

Inquiry: this also became a strategy that helped me overcome many barriers that could have otherwise stopped me from being my best. A few days after starting my class, I quickly identified an older student. I questioned him about the German grading system, examination structures, best study practices and didn't fail to ask who the best in the class was. This inquiry was constructive as I got educated on their system, which differed from Nigeria's.

Discipline: I refused to give myself excuses on those freezing mornings when I had to attend lectures at 8:00 am. Instead, I would double every piece of clothing on my body and look more like an "Eskimo". Fun fact, this was how my friend described me when I shared one of my first pictures taken in Augsburg, Germany.

My experience from my master's studies helped me to quickly integrate into my PhD programme between Germany and France.

During my PhD studies, I was welcomed with the apparent fact that "PhD research is not an extended master thesis."

How then did I adapt to the new city of Karlsruhe, Germany, a new research group both in KIT and the University of Bordeaux and ended up winning the 2020 PhD Sustainable Chemistry thesis award from the German Chemical Society?

The following strategies were instrumental in how I adapted and thrived in my PhD research environments.

Not overwhelmed: I consciously made effort not to be overwhelmed by the sheer broadness of what a PhD thesis should be. I remember the first presentation I attended while at KIT. This presentation was from one of the top PhD candidates; she was just a few weeks to her defence and had published in the leading journals. During her presentation, what kept running through my mind was how someone could accomplish so much work within three to four years? Not being able to dismiss such a thought was enough to scare any new PhD student, I employed my next strategy; identify.

Identify: this was a critical strategy that I quickly adopted at that stage of my PhD life. Here, I quickly identified with people who inspired me or were operating at a level that I wished for myself in the future. After her presentation, I promptly walked up to this fantastic PhD candidate in this specific example. I introduced myself and went on to ask her what advice she could give a fresh PhD candidate like me? This conversation was constructive and also helped calmed my fears of the unknown. However, I didn't stop with her, I took the same question to other older candidates on the team.

Start & learn: this was another essential strategy. The mindset needed to employ this strategy is "not to attempt to cross the bridge before getting to the river." This strategy meant starting the journey before trying to solve the problems that would only show up on the way or might not even show up at all.

Acknowledge: I did my very best not to be dismissive of what I didn't know. Breaking that expectation, I felt others had of me because I was on a full funded scholarship and therefore should know so and so, was vital in adapting to this new environment. I quickly learned that no one expected you to run a Nuclear Magnetic Resonance, Fourier Transformed Infra-Red Spectrophotometer, and other equipments without adequate training.

Communication: When I struggled at the beginning of my PhD research, this strategy became a huge differentiating factor. Being able to explain to my supervisor the actual state of my research despite how "not-so-good" it looked became a fundamental key that unlocked the success of my research.

Collaboration & networking: I quickly identified where I could collaborate with my colleagues. This way, I ended up with 4 out of my 7 PhD research publications borne out of collaboration. In addition, this strategy helped me to build a robust network both internally and externally for my PhD project.

When I moved into my first industry role as a Research Scientist at Procter & Gamble, it was one of the most effortless adaptations. I could attribute this to the fact that I had developed most of the skills required to have a smooth start-up in a multinational company. These skills ranged from team player to collaboration, networking, and leadership.

In the end, most of us would likely find ourselves in a new environment, now or later.

To adapt to any new environment, we need to first remind ourselves of the purpose of being there in the first place. Being clear on our purpose will help develop the resilience required to adapt and thrive. It is equally important that we don't come into a new environment with any "pre-defined thought" on what we expect to see based on hearsay. Experiencing things ourselves will always allow us to make the best judgement.

With millions of people leaving their country of origin to seek greener pastures abroad, the expected outcome for us all is to adapt to our new environment and thrive. However, it might be helpful to recall that we need to go through the process first before thriving. To successfully go through the process, having a mindset that sees beyond our self-actualisation will make a big difference.

As explained in the Holy Bible in Proverbs 11:25, "he who waters will also be watered."

I hope we all adapt and thrive in our new environments by applying these tips and more.

32
No Victim Card to Play

There is no doubt that life has dealt us with different cards. For example, just being born at a particular time and place could have a tremendous impact on our chances of survival. We can't deny this fact no matter how much we try. On the other hand, not being able to influence where we are born and background could quickly put us as victims. I have been repeatedly asked how my Nigerian educational background impacted my postgraduate studies abroad.

My response is usually that "if you did well here, you will do well there."

Let me expand this mindset, starting with the words of one of my school teachers, "to be able to face tomorrow's challenge, we need to face today's challenges first." I like this ideology because it gives us the power to decide, from where we stand, in the present and not in the future. This consciousness takes away the burden of being victims of our circumstances. Yes, we didn't choose where we were born, our environment or the education quality available. But we have the ability to chart our own path. Like the words of one of the most outstanding United States of America presidents, Abraham Lincoln, "the best way to predict the future is to create it." Creating our future starts from our present. Our intentionality on making calculated choices that are designed to lead us to the future of our dreams is a key enabler on what differentiates us from others.

The importance of assessing our future performance based on our past experiences is the foundation of behavioural or situational-based interviews. The outcome of such an interview is that the employer can rate or predict your future actions based on how you handled similar tasks or challenges in the past.

Therefore, looking at how you performed academically during your undergraduate studies is a good litmus test on how you will perform in a postgraduate studies abroad.

Thus, a few months ago, I had to step in to contribute during a heated discussion on LinkedIn. The discussion centred on how inadequate developing country universities prepare their students for postgraduate studies in more developed countries. In my contribution to this discussion, and using Nigeria as an example, I positioned that successive governments have shown a low priority on education funding. The outcome is a lack of adequate research facilities to train her teeming youths. Nevertheless, that is *Nigeria's* inadequacies and not *Nigerians*. Why do I make this distinction? The reason is simple; take a survey of Nigerians who ventured out of the country and deduce their academic achievements during this period. The majority excel in their academic pursuit and have been considered one of the most successful immigrants in the USA.

This fact brings me to the question, does playing the victim card of where we are coming from necessary to take us to where we want to be? There is no doubt that the success of Nigerians abroad is a function of their hard work. Thus, we see a strong correlation with the performance of most of these successful Nigerians abroad while they were still in Nigeria. Hence, if they did well in Nigeria with all the inadequacies involved, they usually repeated such feats abroad when provided with world-class facilities.

There is no room for playing the victim or excuse card in this present world. Excuse cards aimed at explaining why you don't know or have appropriate knowledge about a subject because your professor did not teach you. Take off such cards and start searching. With the abundance of resources online, you do not allow where you are coming from to determine who or where you can be.

Finally, succeeding anywhere is usually a function of how you address your challenge. Of course, these challenges might be different when studying in your home country or abroad. Still, they share a similar trait, and your part is to overcome them. Yes, our various home countries might have serious inadequacies that could mean we need to do more to become our dream. As a Nigerian, I refused to let my educational background stop me from delivering my best during my graduate studies. By refusing to be a victim of my environment and background, I focused on creating my future. Knowing how I handled the challenges then as a Nigerian undergraduate was paramount in preparing me to handle future challenges when I moved to Europe. By doing well in Nigeria, it was no surprise that I repeated a similar feat in Europe.

So how do you plan to chart your future path irrespective of what cards life has dealt you?

33
Lose Not Sight of the Bigger Picture: The Domino Effect

How can we keep the bigger picture in sight if we cannot paint it? How do we understand that the opportunities we didn't get today are all meant to prepare us for a bigger opportunity or aimed at redirecting us? How can we appreciate that the yearly rejections we get for our scholarship applications are meant to reposition us to align with our future? How do we know if God uses the delay we are facing to prepare us for our destined future? These are questions that keep coming to mind when I look back at my own experience during my scholarship journey experience especially on the ones I didn't get and how this all added up to get me to where I am today.

As described in the chapter on my scholarship journey, I was placed on reserved list for the Erasmus Mundus Scholarship for Functional Advanced Materials Engineering (FAME). Being among the top on the reserved list gave me the opportunity to be nominated for an alternative funding AMADEUs LabEX (Advanced Materials by Design Laboratory of Excellence) to be able to participate in the program.

Unlike the Erasmus Mundus Scholarship that was worth, at this time, 43,000 euros for two years; the AMADEUs LabEx was 18,000 euros for the same duration. Eventually, I was selected with two other candidates to receive this funding. The 18,000 euros funding was split as follows; 8,000 euros for tuition fee (4,000 euros per year) and 10,000 euros as a stipend for two years.

At this point, I was a Graduate Assistant at the Department of Chemistry, Federal University of Technology Owerri (FUTO). When I got this funding, I discussed it with my academic mentor. I explained to him that the offer was insufficient to cover my cost of living. He suggested that I apply for TETFund (Tertiary Education Trust Fund; a Nigerian government funding to support tertiary education) to cover this additional cost. However, the probability of getting this funding was very low because I had just been a university staff for less than two months.

Nevertheless, I built up the courage and applied, followed it up with my Head of Department, Dean of Faculty and DVC (Deputy Vice-Chancellor) Academics. Once my application was at the DVC Academic's office, I reached out to my church chaplain, who helped put in good words about me to the DVC Academics. I had initially requested four million naira (19,000 euros equivalence then). The DVC Academics approved half of it (two million naira; 9,500 euros), which was still quite a big surprise to all. I remember standing at the DVC's office after receiving the approval. Everyone was shocked, and in their disbelief, asked how this was possible. "Well, I am a child of destiny," I replied. When the final approval came from TETFund, that amount was increased to three million four hundred thousand naira (about 16,000 euros). To add a cherry on the cake, I also got approval for study leave with pay that translated to about five hundred euros monthly. Eventually, my monthly stipend was above what anyone with the Erasmus Mundus Scholarship was getting. Keep in mind that this would not have been possible if I got the Erasmus Mundus Scholarship in the first place.

While I got a better overall package than my peers, I also got something even more; let me explain. One of the main conditions of receiving the AMADEUs LabEx funding was to complete my M2 (second-year master) at the University of Bordeaux. As a rule with Erasmus Mundus Programs, you cannot complete the studies in one country since mobility is an essential deliverable. The FAME masters then had two options of starting the M1, University of Grenoble, France and University of Augsburg, Germany. Usually, students are distributed between these two starting universities. After the first year, the students are assigned, depending on their interest, between the other partner universities within four countries. My path was already selected as a LabEx funding recipient. The first year had to be at the University of Augsburg, Germany and the second year at the University of Bordeaux, France. And this is where it got interesting; I didn't have to deal with the *choice problem* of which university to go after the first year. Interestingly, the University of Bordeaux had the most substantial Chemistry graduate program in the consortium and was also the leading campus responsible for collaborating many of the Erasmus Mundus Programs which helped broaden my network.

What is the bigger picture I want to paint here, you might ask?

As I look back, going to the University of Bordeaux was pivotal to all the following next steps; *the domino effect* that resulted in where I am at the moment. How did this unfold?

Firstly, by going to the University of Bordeaux, I was able to join an excellent laboratory, Laboratoire de Chimie des Polymères Organiques (LCPO), for my master's internship.

Secondly, because I joined the LCPO for my master's internship, I impressed my supervisors, who gave good feedback to the laboratory director, who was one of the co-supervisors for the prestigious Marie-Curie ITN PhD project I had applied.

Thirdly, the laboratory director gave a solid recommendation about me to the co-supervisor and host professor for this PhD position, which led him to schedule an interview with me.

Fourthly, I got selected for this prestigious double PhD position out of the over one hundred candidates!

Furthermore, by doing this particular PhD project, I contributed significantly to this area of research with seven peer-reviewed publications (five as the first author). In addition, I presented at over twenty different conferences/workshops in over seven countries. Also collaborated with seven other laboratories spread across Germany, France, and Finland, attended yearly summer schools across France, Portugal and Luxembourg, and graduated with a double PhD degree. To top it all, I received the 2020 award for best PhD thesis on Sustainable Chemistry from the German Chemical Society (GDCh).

The domino effect did not end there.

Additionally, Karlsruhe Institute of Technology (KIT), being one of the key universities for recruitment for Procter & Gamble, gave me visibility to the company. Therefore, I applied and got accepted into the PhD Seminar organised by the company. After this seminar, and not long after, I got called one afternoon for an impromptu interview with P&G which resulted to receiving a permanent position, barely three months after defending my PhD.

After going through this chapter, you might ask if I saw the bigger picture of not getting the Erasmus Mundus Scholarship? To which I would sincerely respond that I did not. I couldn't have imagined all this linked-outcome without actually being at this very spot today, where I can look back and appreciate how it all added up.

Looking at the bigger picture implies that we are not in a hurry to conclude on our future (unknown) by simply looking at our current situation. When I didn't get the Erasmus Mundus Scholarship, I felt disappointed. When the offer from LabEx came in, which was indeed not enough to support my studies, I still couldn't factor how this was a better alternative. When I submitted my TETFund application, many colleagues thought I was nought. "What sort of exuberance?" they asked since I had just been a staff member for less than two months. I even pushed my limit by applying for a study leave with pay! These were all approved. The summary here is that none of these would have been possible if I had gotten the *one yes* from

Erasmus Mundus Scholarship. Today, I have directly and indirectly mentored over fifty graduates to win this same scholarship.

I hope this chapter helps you develop the resilience to keep the bigger picture in sight as you go through each rejection or delay. Keeping the bigger picture in sight is a vital growth mindset skill that allows us to be cautious and not to be satisfied by short-cuts or easy-going solutions that can only guarantee immediate satisfaction; the now or never mentality.

Yes, we might not have the bigger picture as a concrete painting hanging on our walls, but we can paint it in our minds, which is a practical demonstration of HOPE. Keeping sight of that bigger picture will allow us to go through the challenges, rejections, disappointments that come with life without giving up. By going through life with such a positive mindset, we develop resilience, which will enable us to be more daring and determined, never to give up till we can sit back and physically paint that bigger picture because it has come true.

34
Not Easy: Experience from My PhD Journey

A well-structured CV and a profile with a series of winnings all seem too easy once put on paper. As a trained Chemist, one of the jokes we usually make is that every chemical reaction looks so easy once put on paper, but when you are in the laboratory, then reality sets. For example, when we look at the world record achieved by Usain Bolt in the 100m race at the Olympics, what is not visible during those sub 10 seconds of racing the 100m are the many hours per day over many years that he practised to be able to achieve this feat. Little wonder someone once looked at my profile on LinkedIn and commented that my life seems to have been very easy. But once we investigate the details, open the sacrifices made to achieve those results, we begin to appreciate what it took, and we come to one conclusion, "not easy."

Life is not meant to be easy, and there is no thrill to live without going through the various challenges that come our way. I consider my PhD research experience a great example. The summary of my PhD was that I graduated within a record time of three years to obtain a double PhD degree, published seven research articles, and, to crown it all, received the 2020 best PhD award from the German Chemical Society on Sustainable Chemistry. "The devil is in the details," goes an old saying, and in my opinion, looking at the details behind this feat is more interesting.

I started my PhD research on the 1st of February, 2016. I was the last to commence my thesis out of the fifteen candidates accepted to the Marie-Curie EJD-FunMat (European Joint Doctoral in Functional Materials). First, there was a delay in finalising my PhD contract between KIT-Germany and the University of Bordeaux, France. When this was finally ready in November 2015, the subsequent delay came from the German consulate in Nigeria. Finally, I arrived in Germany by the end of January 2016, and the next day I was already in the laboratory. After being introduced to my supervisor and given a tour, safety training, and assigned a fume hood, I was ready to start. Almost immediately, I started with my first reactions. My project was on developing sustainable approaches for making materials from cellulose. The other aspect involved demonstrating the recycling of the ionic liquid solvent used in this cellulose valorisation using supercritical CO_2. This second aspect of the work was to be carried out at the University of Bordeaux, while the first aspect was at KIT-Germany. My project idea was conceived based on the work done during an MSc thesis by one of the students in the KIT group. In her thesis, she demonstrated the use of beta-cyclodextrin in multicomponent reactions (Ugi five component reaction; Ugi-5CR) with the help of CO_2. The interest with this work, when applied to cellulose, was that it would allow us to achieve multiple functionalities on cellulose in one step and might open the door to the development of functional-target material or functionality-on-demand cellulose materials.

The first experiments I did aimed to transfer the success of the reaction with beta-cyclodextrin to cellulose, which was obviously expected to be more challenging. One of these challenges was the insolubility of cellulose in the most common solvents; hence, I was exploring the use of ionic liquids, a special type of solvent for cellulose. Another colleague in the team was already working on cellulose derivatisation using ionic liquids and provided me with the needed guidance on what to do. About one week into my research, and to the surprise of almost everyone, I was able to show some level of modification on cellulose. How did you manage this? We thought it would take months to get to any level of modification, they wondered. After two weeks, I was off to the EJD-FunMat summer school in Bordeaux, France. The first-year candidates like me had 5 minutes to present their research work, whereas the older candidates had 10 minutes to discuss their research progress. Hence, the audience was surprised when I presented my first results; a Fourier Transformed Infra-red (FT-IR) spectra comparison between cellulose and the modified cellulose. Their surprise was justifiable considering that some of my other colleagues who had started back in October-September 2015 didn't have much result to share at that point. When I came back from summer school, my supervisor and I discussed the various optimisation and characterisation methods I could explore, so we could start organising the data for a possible publication.

Building on my initial early success, I returned to the laboratory with the expectation that I would optimise the reaction within a few weeks. But, unfortunately, I could not have been more wrong as after five months and struggling to optimise my reactions, I received the shock of my research life.

On that fateful morning, I had gone to the laboratory as usual and noticed that my final products showed some colour variation within the same batch. However, when I did an FT-IR measurement on the coloured part, the spectrum looked different compared to that from the non-coloured part. What could this mean? I wondered because I had followed the same purification steps as employed by the colleague that worked on beta-cyclodextrin. That morning, instead of washing my product with only ethanol and ethyl acetate, I decided to wash it using methanol; the obtained product was homogenous and showed no colour variation. Then I took an FT-IR measurement, and boom—the result showed only pure cellulose peaks, no modification!

I thought I was dreaming and repeated the experiment. This time, after washing the product with methanol, I collected the extract from the methanol phase and determined the functional group present through FT-IR measurement. My fear was finally confirmed; the supposed modification I had seen over the past months had been a side reaction that was not attached to cellulose. To make sure this was not peculiar to cellulose, I requested my colleague who worked on beta-cyclodextrin to attempt a methanol-washing of her final modified product. The outcome was the same; the modification was not on the substrate! My worst fear of failing when I started my PhD had finally come to pass. I was devastated, felt helpless and lost!

When I went to my supervisor that morning, I could barely lift my feet off the ground, shivering and shaking, unsure how he would receive this shocking news. I imagined the disappointment on his face as he wondered why he hired me out of over a hundred candidates that applied for this position. I had done a mental calculation of the cost of chemicals used for the over fifty experiments I had done by that time, which made me feel even worse. I felt so stupid for celebrating that I was succeeding in the first place. I can't remember ever feeling that low in my life. After explaining the situation to my supervisor, he looked up at me and said one of the most soothing words I have ever heard, "Kenny, a failed experiment is not a failed life, we are even lucky you discovered this very early, and this could give you a paragraph or two in your final thesis." I left his office convinced that, there could be no successful thesis without a supportive supervisor. When I got home that evening, I did a video in which I reaffirmed to myself with the following words: "I am the best candidate to deliver this project successfully; I do not see anyone better than myself that can bring this project to a successful completion." After that, I was more confident and ready for whatever my PhD research brought.

This supposed setback eventually became a blessing to me. Upon carrying out a root cause analysis, I identified the ionic liquid being used as the cause for the observed side reaction. With these facts, I started exploring another solvent system which led me to CO_2 switchable solvent systems. All thanks to my colleague who came across this solvent system while contributing to a review article. Within six months of working on this new solvent system, I had two publications, with one as first author. My research pushed the boundary of this relatively novel solvent system, and I ended up with seven peer-reviewed publications (five as the first author).

Interestingly, six of my articles were already published before my PhD defence on the 4th of February 2019 (exactly three years from when I started). My PhD jury did not hesitate to commend me on the level of diversity in my work which covered a broad range from cellulose solvent system development to solubilisation, derivatisation, and eventual cellulose regeneration. More so, I was able to collaborate with five other laboratories across Finland, Germany and France that were not part of the project. Even more exciting was that I attended and presented at over twenty international conferences/workshops/Science fairs across Europe and the USA and won numerous awards. In May 2019, I presented to an audience of over 1,300 people at the Germany finals of the FAMELAB Science communication competition after emerging among the two winners from the regional finals in Karlsruhe, Germany. My thesis eventually won the 2020 PhD Award on Sustainable Chemistry from the German Chemical Society (GDCh).

In retrospect, all this would likely not have been possible if I did not experience the setback and massive failure earlier on.

This experience further show that the challenges, hard work, and disappointments behind our success are not usually apparent by just looking at our profiles. I hope this chapter helps us not lose hope when we pass through our challenges because we are getting *carried away* by those who have passed that phase and are now celebrating the results. Remember that results are a product of the process; therefore, never forget to celebrate the process. Appreciate the road you are currently travelling even before getting to the destination. While waiting to reach that thousandth miles, enjoy and celebrate those small steps you are taking today that will eventually add to the thousand miles. By structuring your mind in this way, you wouldn't lose focus because you have not *arrived* but will be happy with your daily progress. You will not feel you are late because you know for sure your time will come, and those small steps and sacrifices you are making today towards your goal will eventually bring you to your destination. Eventually, when you build such a mindset, you will not give up because life is not easy. But will face every challenge and failure as they come, knowing that the lessons from these experiences are needed to prepare you for the future of your dream.

THEME 11:
Humility in Success

35
Humility Can Be Learnt

What if you need someone to teach you? This thought kept ringing in my head the whole evening. What if I needed the same assistance my classmates were requesting from me?

Sometime in 2009 while as a third year undergraduate student, two of classmates approached me regarding their challenge in some of our first semester courses. They wanted me to organise tutorials to help them catch up. However, considering that the best location for such a tutorial was about a kilometre from where I lived, I didn't think it was feasible.

When I got home that evening, I remembered an experience I had a few years earlier while in high school. We were given an assignment in Further Mathematics that was due to be submitted that day. I spent the entire weekend trying to solve it but to no avail. I imagined the depth of the problem I would land myself into, knowing that our Further Mathematics teacher was very unforgiving. Not completing your assignment was among the most significant crime you could commit in his eyes. It was never in my nature to copy from my classmates which only worsened my predicament. On the submission D-day, I got to school very earlier than usual, hoping to find someone who had done the assignment to get help. Unfortunately, the classmates I met were either busy with something else or had given up on the assignment because of its difficulty.

Finally, I approached one of our best mathematician in class to seek help. When I showed him the question, he looked at it for a few minutes in silence and wrote the answer. I had landed on the bridge of confusion. He had skipped a lot of steps thanks to calculating in his mind. I stared in disbelief at how he could solve the question I had struggled with all weekend. "How did you do it? Please help me outline the steps," I persisted as if my life depended on understanding how he solved the assignment.

He was very kind to take me through the steps of the answer he got, and I left very excitedly, knowing that I had narrowly escaped the grave punishment from my unforgiving teacher.

And here I was a few years down memory lane when two classmates needed my help. Yet, despite how inconvenient it was, I could still relate to the uneasy feeling of difficulty they were facing like I felt when I needed help on my Further Mathematics assignment.

I resolved to help them even when it meant I had to walk about one kilometre, three times a week for the tutorial. The outcome was fantastic, and there was nothing more pleasing than seeing the warm smiles on their faces while they received their semester results. It was their best semester result by far. I had this deep inner joy of fulfilment that I couldn't explain in words. My passion for helping others only grew stronger after this incident.

You might ask how humility came into the picture.

In my opinion, humility is built on the foundation of our self-incompleteness; we need others to become our dream, our future. When we fully understand this, we will never take anyone for granted. Reflecting on my personal experience, I often found myself amongst the best students in all levels of my educational pursuit from primary school through my PhD studies. During these long years of studying, I noticed a trend that occurred to me; I did woefully in my exams when I felt I knew enough. Humility allows us to help others not for what they can offer but because we also need to be supported. The same way I approached my classmate in high school and requested help for my Further Mathematics assignment is the same way I see others who come to me for assistance. Do you think you will need help from others? If yes, then never forget to extend the same assistance to others.

Furthermore, humility allows us to appreciate that we don't and can't know everything. Humility allows us to build a vital networking skill that enables us to leverage the strength of others in the quest towards achieving our goals. In addition, humility means treating everyone with respect irrespective of their social class, educational level, and financial strength.

Some people view humility as weaknesses, but in reality, being humble amidst the pursuit of success is the highest form of strength. As you progress on the ladder of success in attaining greater heights, staying humble becomes more difficult. I am at the school of humility, still learning.

Let's keep recognising that wherever we are now was not by our making alone; the gift of people empowered us to that point. More so, when we accept that there is still room for growth, we are sure to stay humble.

Therefore, let us learn the art of humility.

36

Remember Yesterday

"I received the worst education ever!" he commented. I was still trying to process what experiences he must have had to trigger such expression, and voila! Another person dropped his comment stating how unfortunate he was to have completed his undergraduate studies in Nigeria. "What is going on here?" I pondered. Most of the commenters had encountered similar challenges. Therefore did not mind baring it all on the social media post about obtaining international scholarships with a Nigerian graduate certificate, especially those commenting from Europe and North America. As they freely expressed their frustration from past experiences, one thing was clear. Provided they had a Nigerian undergraduate certificate and, no matter how inconsequential, did play a pivotal role in their international scholarship win!

Over the years, I have realised that we quickly forget yesterday when we get to tomorrow. My father once said, "forgetting where you are coming from is a sure recipe for disaster." I could not agree less. In this case, it is impossible to erase our first teacher. Yet, despite the hurdles and pain, we push even harder and stay believing.

Essential requirements for an international scholarship application include a university degree certificate, academic transcript, motivation letter/statement of purpose, curriculum vitae and recommendation letters. It is thus evident that one cannot boycott an undergraduate degree. There is no argument that most Nigerian public universities, including those in many developing countries, are seriously lagging compared to their counterparts in the USA and Europe. However, it is impossible to rate it as very poor as it has produced millions of outstanding students and professionals worldwide. The real question is: how does a bad rating better the educational system? Again, reducing the quality of your degree certificate to the barest minimum is simply an indirect way of telling the scholarship selection committee that you are underserving of such a scholarship. It is no longer the country or school but you. Are you incapable of defending what you studied?

Another perspective is considering what impact these bad ratings have on the younger generation of people coming after you? What will be their fate if the scholarship selection committee draws conclusions based on social media posts and comments that are downgrading the Nigerian or developing countries educational system/certificate?

When I moved to Germany for my masters in 2013, I remember the first classes I took on Material Physics. Almost everything was new, whereas my European counterparts all appeared to have a strong background in the course already. That day, I decided to do all that it would take to catch up, even if it meant sleeping in the library. I meant every word and followed with actions. Eventually, I ended up with one of the best grades in my class on the course. My undergraduate education at the Federal University of Technology, Owerri, Nigeria, might not have taught me the prerequisite to seamlessly take this graduate course at the University of Augsburg, Germany. However, it did teach me resilience, persistence, and ruggedness. As an undergraduate student, I remember waking very early to be in class by 6:30 am for a lecture that only started at 8:30 am, so that I could sit in front of the usually crowded class. It was a norm, not only for me but anyone very interested in hearing and understanding the lecturer. In a lecture hall of over three hundred students, it was difficult to grasp all taught without a sound system/microphone. I remember running from one end of the campus to another, covering hundreds of metres in between lectures. I usually ended up trekking several kilometres in a day, all in a bid to attend my courses at different locations. Do I begin to narrate the many verification exercises while queuing under the sun? I had to study many nights with candle lights or kerosene lamps because there was no electricity supply. What about the mental torment from dealing with sadist lecturers who did not hide their faces in shame as they boast that no one in the class can make an *A grade* in their course. I am sure that these experiences are not peculiar to me but to most students who graduated from a Nigerian or other developing country's public university. Alas, despite all these, we succeeded!

Sincerely, most of the things I had to do or put up during my undergraduate study helped me deal with even more significant challenges during my postgraduate studies in Europe and in my current professional career.

So what is my advice to international scholars that engage in such debates especially in public spaces? Before engaging in conversations that downgrade the Nigerian undergraduate degree certificate or your home country degree, which you bear and probably served as the basis for the scholarship you received, think it over. Constructive criticisms would do a lot to identify how to address those challenges faced as an undergraduate and would, in turn, do much good. Also, consider that your reactions might discourage the next person in diverse ways. Therefore, what would be ideal moving forward is to spread positive energy and create support.

Thus, we must remember yesterday in everything we do.

THEME 12:
Till We All Win

37
Not Again: The Experience That Redefined Winning for Me

"Kelechukwu Nnabuike, 76%" The geography teacher took another look at my script as I approached him. How did you manage to get such a high score? He asked, looking even more surprised. I was the only one in the class to pass Geography in our ordinary level GCE mock examination at the Presbyterian Comprehensive High School (PCHS) Kumbo.

A similar scenario played out when our Economics and Biology results were released, and I came out with a 75% and 90% score, respectively. Again, the fact that I had excelled in these subjects were extraordinarily noticeable because over 90% of the class scored below 50%.

Typically, one would expect that I would be so excited about my remarkable performance. But, No, the reverse was the case. I was rather sad. This is not to rule out that I was happy with my result deep down, but then I could not bring myself to celebrate under such circumstances. At this point, I was made to remember the teachings of Apostle Paul in Philippians 2:2, where he admonished that we should be like-minded with each other and love one another.

After much thinking and feeling, I concluded that winning alone was rather boring and lonely. But then, again, occupying that winner position alone rid me of the ability to grow. Hence, I redirected my focus towards identifying ways to help my classmates share the same win.

It is also important to understand that at this point, I was pained by a police arrest a few years earlier, coupled with the constant discrimination I was experiencing fueled a feeling of dislike for Cameroon as a country. Yet, I looked beyond what I was passing through to seek ways through which I could help my Cameroonian classmates to win with me.

Owing to my new decision, I engaged my classmates in daily tutorials. This was the first time I experimented with how a study group approach could help achieve a collective win. It was heart-warming to see my study mates smile as they shared how the group studying helped them scale through their exams. When the final GCE O-level results were released, my study group did exceptionally well.

In addition to achieving a collective win with my classmates, I didn't initially realise that I was also learning and growing through this approach.

Despite not being at the top of my class when I got to high school, I reapplied study group approach. The group was made up of was five people with me inclusive. We studied together after classes and on weekends. Each person was expected to research a topic in an assigned subject and share it with the team. This was an example of a "divide and conquer" approach that eventually helped us as a group to cover most of the examination curriculum within a short period.

When the advanced level GCE examination results were announced, my group achieved a 100% pass! I remember one of them approached me after the results were out with tears in her eyes, saying that she wouldn't have made it without my support. It was the team support, I quickly interjected. I didn't do it alone; we did it as a team.

I feel delighted seeing how much difference the study group approach helped me *carry along* my classmates to achieve a collective win.

I do not doubt that *via* intentional living, we can train out mindset, to not be afraid of the success of others, to not withhold opportunities to others simply because it doesn't benefit us, to realise that the winning of others doesn't mean we are losing. In addition, I believe that till that time when everyone has won, when everyone is living a worthwhile life, till that time comes, let no one feel that they have indeed won. I have been asked repeatedly whether such a time will ever come. My response has been that if each person can develop such a consciousness, then extending our help to others will gradually become a task we put onto ourselves each day we walk out the door. With such a mindset, we would not sit back to relax because we feel we have *arrived*, whereas millions are struggling to get what we can offer.

This is why I am a big advocate and promoted the now-famous phrase and title of this book "till we all win, we are all a work in progress."

Not again-should we relax on our *win* when others struggle and need our help to move to their next phase.

38
Where My Loyalty Lies

I have shared in the preceding chapter how I developed & successfully applied the study group approach towards achieving a collective win. Long after secondary school and high school, that unifying winning mindset has remained with me. Yet, I noticed that the group study approach is not applicable in all scenarios in driving a collective win. Take as an example during a final year undergraduate course in which my classmates could not be helped through group study alone. Irrespective of how many hours of tutorials I organised, they were not confident enough to pass the course being handled by the assigned professor. His style of teaching was a turn-off for them. I found myself paradoxically choosing between individual gain and class-gain.

Here is how this experience unfolded.

As a final year student, my class took a course on Synthetic Methods in Organic Chemistry that a *no-nonsense professor* was assigned. This professor equally doubled as my academic mentor, having been opportune to know him since my second year at the university.

The majority of the class panicked as they were sure they would not pass the course and risk having an extra semester if this assigned professor was not removed. Over 99% of the class members planned a protest to the HOD (Head of the department) to prevent risking an additional semester.

Upon taking their stance, I was approached by many of my classmates, requesting that I partake in the protest. "KC, you know if this professor takes this course, many of us will fail and might have an additional semester." I understood their position, but I was anxious about joining them, especially considering the risk the protest would pose on my excellent mentorship relationship with this professor. The decision line was clear; keep my excellent relationship with the professor by not joining the protest or join the protest with over 99% of my class, thereby helping them graduate but risk losing the relationship with my academic mentor.

It certainly wasn't an easy decision to make, and I battled with it for some time. But, eventually, I concluded that I did not want to graduate alone, nor did I want to celebrate my graduation when many of my classmates couldn't. Therefore, if taking a stand with the rest could help foster the department to listen to their plight, I was willing to support them.

The D-day came, nearly the entire class boycotted, including me. I was overwhelmed seeing the joy on their faces, pleased that their best student joined them to seek a common good. The protest indeed made a difference as the HOD decided to assign a second professor who handled the practical part of the course. This new arrangement helped many of my classmates to pass the course. So it was no surprise on our graduation day, the enormous celebration that took place with my classmates celebrating the achievement of my first class honours as theirs. It indeed was heart-warming.

Taking the side of class gain instead of personal gain and seeing its positive impact helped me recognise and re-consolidate the "we all win" mentality.

Yes, "till we all win" might sound like a brag, a branding gimmick or, better still, a half conceived effort at taking the unsuspecting on a fairy tale. However, I have come to the fact that having an "all-win" mentality doesn't deny anyone the chance to succeed. Just as Malcolm X puts it, "when *We* replace *I*, *Ill*ness becomes *Well*ness."

If I could go back in history to this same incident, I would still choose class-gain over self-gain. However, if we are to glance at the bigger picture, I was also part of the class gain. Just as a tree, no matter how elegant it is, cannot make a forest, we also need people around us on our journey through life.

Developing a mentality that supports a "win for all" from my viewpoint is the sole requirement of what it takes to build a sustainable society, and this is where my loyalty lies.

When winning is not centred on the mentality that *the winner takes it all*, we begin to seek more synergetic solutions to the rising problems we face daily. But, again, no singular tree can make a forest, the same way no singular person can make a community. The earlier we realise that we need others to go far, the closer we are to living a life of significant impact.

Now you know where my loyalty lies, and my goal remains not to win alone in any environment I find myself in.

39
The Place of Coaching and Mentoring

In addition to the study group approach, pitching our loyalty on the side of an *all-win* instead of *I-win*, coaching & mentorship can equally give us the opportunity to birth a *till we all win* society.

Let me share two experiences showing how coaching and mentorship could rekindle hope.

It was high school, and I was sitting in class reading when I got tapped on the shoulder. I looked over and saw my classmate and friend, with tears in his eyes. "KC, I am completely lost, and I don't see myself passing this Biology," he said to me in between sobbing.

This was happening just a few months before the Advanced level GCE examinations. Among all the subjects we were to sit for, Biology was the most voluminous. The subject curriculum was so broad that it would take more than a year to go through it thoroughly. So when this classmate came to me to express his frustration, I could very much relate. What even made this a dicey situation was that we were already getting close to the exams, and I understood that if he felt this way, it could potentially affect his performance in the other subjects. This disaster was waiting to happen if we did nothing to avert it on time.

The first thing I did was ask him to write down the topics he was yet to cover in Biology. Next, I worked with him to set up an efficient study plan that ran for three months. The timetable was very clear and concise, and I allotted time for each topic he was yet to cover. Creating such a very detailed timetable was not an easy task because it involved going through the content of each topic to be able to allocate the required time needed to complete such. It was also crucial not to work with any assumption; hence, I had him confirm how much time he thought he needed for a given topic before entering it on the timetable.

In addition, the study plan also had to factor in the other four subjects that he was to take in the GCE A-level examination. In the end, we had a very detailed study plan, and the next step was to ensure we tracked his progress daily. As the weeks progressed, he felt more and more confident and relaxed. The insurmountable mountain that stood before him gradually became plain, and he didn't hide his excitement each time we reviewed his progress. The exams finally came, and when the results were out, he passed all five subjects, even making one of his best grades in Biology.

The second example I like to narrate occurred when I encountered another basically hopeless student when I was an undergraduate student a few years down the road of this first example. This hopeless student was standing outside the office of the head of the chemistry department, crying. It turned out that he had just gotten his first-year results and had been told by the course advisor that his poor grades meant he didn't stand a chance of graduating any time soon. Further inquiry showed he had made about 3Fs, which meant he had to carry over these courses.

The issue here was not that he had failed these courses, but because the course advisor whose responsibility was to act as a mentor and coach to their students made this student see that he had no hope in continuing.

As you can imagine, one of the saddest things that can happen is when the person who should help, give you hope becomes the same person who takes it away. I took some time to go through his results, showed him the impact of the carryovers, and it was clear that he felt much better when we were done. I made him understand that even though this might lead to an extra semester, it doesn't mean that's the end of the world. I pointed out that his classmates were graduating before him was not enough to quit on his dreams.

I advised him to find someone in his class who could help him understand those areas he was facing challenges in and dedicate more time to his studies. In summary, I made him see that there was hope, which was what counted the most. I followed up with him over the years, and recently I saw his update on Facebook and was indeed very happy to know that he was pulling weight in an area where he has the most interest. He might not have finished practising the Chemistry course he studied as an undergraduate, but today he is making a difference in his way.

We should never write people off based on today's experience because tomorrow is a mystery.

These two examples showed me the importance of coaching and mentoring even when I didn't have the right words for what I was doing. As we navigate the uncertainties that characterise this life, the importance of coaching and mentoring shouldn't be taken for granted. We need someone to look at things from different perspectives and help us draft a working document towards that future, we hope. It doesn't have to be a one-on-one conversation; you can also be coached or mentored by following someone whose life inspires you on various social media platforms. By looking at how they handled their experiences, studying and engaging on their social media platforms, reading their posts/books will help you develop a working plan. There is no faster way of going into your future than learning from someone already ahead in that direction.

These experiences played a big part in the overall reason I founded DEKEMP (Dr KC Mentorship Platform) in June 2019. I understood that regardless of their excellent performance, graduate students will struggle without direction.

Like the experiences I just shared about my high school friend and the Chemistry undergraduate student I met at FUTO, without enabling them to see hope despite what they were passing through, it would have been tough for them to go through life with a positive mindset. Without a positive mindset, such a challenge or obstacle could have become a complete block to their will to keep pushing.

Coaching and mentorship provides options and practical experiences on how best to handle challenges and obstacles that come our way based on the experiences of these mentors/coaches. As the old saying goes, "experience is the best teacher." Therefore, it is best to learn from those who have gone ahead of us.

40
The Culture of Togetherness: DEKEMP and Beyond

As a secondary school student, I experimented with the group study approach towards achieving a collective win. This approach's overwhelming success made me fall in love with the *all-win* mindset. Thus, as an undergraduate, when faced with a paradox to choose between personal gain and class gain, my loyalty unequivocally opted for class gain. Upon graduation, I wondered how I could bring in such a mindset to drive collective goals, especially when I wasn't longer a student.

At this point, I wondered if mentorship & coaching could be the medium through which I could broadly promote this *all-win* mindset.

So when the opportunity presented itself to lead as the 200-level Industrial Chemistry class advisor, I jumped at it with both hands. "Yes," I said to myself. "It was time to experiment if coaching could be used as a tool towards achieving a collective win."

This opportunity presented itself when I joined the Federal University of Technology Owerri as a Graduate Assistant in April 2013. The 200-level class advisor had just gone on maternity leave. I was assigned to step in as her replacement.

The first-year results of the class had just been released when I took over this role. As the course advisor, part of my responsibility was to give students their results verbally. This task was not easy as many students left my office sad and disappointed by their performance.

This set of disappointed students reminded me of my classmates at PCHS Kumbo years earlier. The same look of sadness that inspired me then to initiate the group study approach to help achieve a collective win as narrated in the previous chapter of this book.

I felt this opportunity was the perfect moment to experiment how coaching could give my students hope of a better future and promote the collective win mindset.

The following week I organised a class meeting and allowed them to share their feedback from the previous exams. "What reason would you say contributed to your poor performance?" I asked. Many of them pointed to all other reasons but themselves. "It was the Mathematics department; they don't like Chemistry department students," one of them said. "We have been told that Chemistry is a difficult department to graduate with good grades," another chipped in. "Since you have pointed to many reasons you have no control over, how then are you going to make a better result?" I asked. There was silence.

The connection with my students was very personal to me. I could see that they were potential high-flyer graduates even when they didn't believe in their potential anymore. The just-released semester results had taken a critical inner strength from them; hope. Their performance humbled the overzealousness, confidence and gingerness they came into the university.

That afternoon, I introduced the concept of mindset reset— the importance of taking experience as a lesson and failure as an opportunity to grow. I made them understand that the first step towards mindset reset was taking responsibility for what they did and the outcome, irrespective of how it turned out. I advised that they shouldn't stop at a personal win but look beyond and find how to contribute to collective success. "Some of you are very good at some of the courses your colleagues are struggling with; how about organising tutorials?" I concluded.

After my discussion with them, there was overwhelming applause.

As I left them that afternoon, I could attest that the students felt energised to face their challenges and believed they had what it took to make a good grade from the Chemistry department.

Expectedly, their results improved and a few years down the road, I was one of the happiest person on earth when they briefly included me on their Whatsapp group after their graduation. It was nice to see how my coaching made a positive difference in their individual and class academic performance.

A few years later, after completing my PhD, I wondered how to give back to society. Without having any student or class I could influence directly, I became very active on LinkedIn, mostly posting about scholarship opportunities.

I began receiving lots of interest from graduate students that needed scholarship guidance. To best manage their need and provide the necessary help, on 8th June 2019, I founded DEKEMP. DEKEMP was founded based on three guiding principles: 1) Till we all win, no one has truly won. 2) Process over results 3) Direction over speed. Through mentorship and coaching, I introduced the all-win mindset, and today this has become the mantra of DEKEMP

From about fifteen mentees during the first months, the number increased to fifty as of late 2019, and currently, we are over three hundred. The platform strived successfully and made an international first impression, with twenty-five members receiving fully funded scholarships in 2020. In the second year of our existence, sixty-one members got full funded scholarships, more than doubled the previous year. As of September 2022, 51 members have equally received fully funded scholarships. This brings the collective award value to over 7.5 million USD.

I have been repeatedly asked what I am doing differently in DEKEMP to achieve such feats within a short time. I usually replied that I work on the mindset of my mentees.

The drive behind DEKEMP has remained hope, which now gives graduate students from financially less buoyant backgrounds something to live for. It is humbling, and I feel grateful for what we have achieved and the brighter future that awaits us as a group.

Running such a mentorship platform almost on a full job basis has not been without hurdles and challenges. However, I am reminded daily of the "why" behind this mentorship platform: hope.

It is *hope* that will keep the undergraduates motivated to study against the backdrop of a society that rewards mediocrity over excellence. It is equally *hope* that will keep the graduate student resilient despite the many rejections of their scholarship application. Call me a preacher of *hope,* and you will not be far from the truth because if there is one most needed thing and at the same time most difficult to give to someone else, it is *hope.*

The togetherness culture I drive within my mentorship platform is imbibed in my firm belief that till we all win, we are all a work in progress. So, in DEKEMP, we believe that we only rise by lifting others. No one needs to be fully *formed* or *made* to start taking others along.

DEKEMP is now a family to me and has provided a home for many graduates and undergraduate students. Our vision is to create an enabling environment through practical mentorship for young people to network, learn and distinctively develop in their diverse career pursuits. Eventually, we want DEKEMP to be recognised as a community of continuously evolving and resilient individuals thriving towards achieving an all-win society.

We aim to achieve this vision through our missions as follows:

1. To build a sustainable mentorship platform/community where members are selfless in enabling the mutual growth of each other.

2. To develop a systematic platform providing relevant and target-specific scholarship information to her members and guide them towards winning international scholarships.

3. To develop individuals with a growth mindset that believes in *Process over Result* and can build resilience, persistence, and ruggedness in pursuing their career goals.

How about taking this all-win mindset to the next level as a way of doing things? That is a culture. So, in summary, DEKEMP is a platform made up of like-minded people where *all-win* is a culture.

So dear reader, I leave you with these questions: what is life if not lived to better society by giving others hope and encouraging those who find no reason to believe in themselves? Would you take the step today towards contributing to an *all-win* society?

AFTERWORD:
My Hope

I hope:

That you remember to lift others as you rise

That you remember the way up is from down

That you will never forget that a journey of a thousand miles starts with the first step

That you will recognise the power of networking

That you remind yourself every morning what an awesome God's creation you are

That you hold onto your dreams no matter what

That you remember to treat everyone with respect, for you never know where you will meet them again

That you stay positive amid every challenge life brings your way

That you appreciate and acknowledge those who were there for you

That your success should humble you just as failure does

That you might lose the battle but still win the war, so stay focused

That failure is not an end in itself but a necessary ingredient of success

That you remember you are not late simply because your peers are making it, your time will come

That you remember, it is direction over speed

That you never forget, it is process over results

Above all, that you should love yourself enough and not try to be someone else

And you should never forget that till we all win, we are all a work in progress.

www.ingramcontent.com/pod-product-compliance
Lightning Source LLC
Chambersburg PA
CBHW022100090426
42743CB00008B/671